Hunger Inc.

'How do you close a food bank – a beacon of what is wrong? By turning it into a shop – preferably a co-op. Kayleigh Garthwaite's ground-breaking work explains why food banks prolong hunger and what must be done.'
—Danny Dorling, School of Geography and the Environment, University of Oxford

'This is the book we need right now, as inequality rages and people across the "wealthy West" turn in ever greater numbers to food banks and other types of food support. Crucially, it gives us something to hang on to: solutions. An absolute must read not just for policymakers, but for everyone.'
—Mary O'Hara, author of *Austerity Bites 10 Years On: A Journey to the Sharp End of Cuts in the UK*

Hunger Inc.

Building Solidarity Beyond
the Food Bank

Kayleigh Garthwaite

Foreword by Kerry Hudson

PLUTO PRESS

For Mam

First published 2026 by Pluto Press
New Wing, Somerset House, Strand, London WC2R 1LA
and Pluto Press, Inc.
1930 Village Center Circle, 3-834, Las Vegas, NV 89134

www.plutobooks.com

British Library Cataloguing in Publication Data
A catalogue record for this book is available from the British Library

ISBN   978 0 7453 5017 2   Paperback
ISBN   978 0 7453 5019 6   PDF
ISBN   978 0 7453 5018 9   EPUB

This book is printed on paper suitable for recycling and made from fully managed and sustained forest sources. Logging, pulping and manufacturing processes are expected to conform to the environmental standards of the country of origin.

Typeset by Stanford DTP Services, Northampton, England

Simultaneously printed in the United Kingdom and United States of America

EU GPSR Authorised Representative
LOGOS EUROPE, 9 rue Nicolas Poussin, 17000, LA ROCHELLE, France
Email: Contact@logoseurope.eu

Contents

Foreword

Kerry Hudson

Summer 1987 was surprisingly sunny for the North of England, and specifically the ex-shipbuilding town of North Shields where I lived. I was six years old and spent my school holidays running around in ever-grubbier, bright yellow dungarees.

I was also six months into living in a homeless hostel with my mum, stepfather and baby sister in a room almost entirely filled by two sets of metal bunk beds. We paid 20p for a shower and used the laundry every fortnight. For food, we had a tabletop freezer and a plug-in frying pan. That summer, we ate mainly frozen sausages and pancakes made from a mix whisked by hand in a plastic jug. I assume both were 'on special'.

In the UK, at that time, benefits were paid to you each Monday by handing in a 'benefits book' of vouchers at the Post Office, which then allowed you to claim your weekly social security. Since those benefits were only ever enough to provide the bare minimum, usually by Thursday or Friday the cupboards were quite literally bare. I vividly remember us sticking our hands down the back of the sofas in the common room – highly inadvisable in that specific homeless hostel, incidentally – to try and find enough coins so we could buy a loaf of bread while my stepdad scanned for anything we might pawn for a few pounds.

As any low-income family will tell you, the summer holidays are hard. Budgeting for the loss of the daily school meal and the price of extra entertainment – even if that's just an ice-lolly here and there – will hit hard when families are already stretched to breaking point. Our family had a variety of other interconnected problems: a lack of cooking and food storage facilities, an unstable, sometimes unsafe, home and parents with mental health and substance abuse problems. For us, summer holidays were a tightrope of resilience; our own personal 'Hunger Games' if you will.

When our desperation was absolute, my mum would go to the social security offices, 'The Social' as she somewhat ironically called it. There we would sit waiting, sometimes for many hours, to explain our plight to an administration officer behind a glass window, usually indifferent at best, wait some more, and then eventually be given a cheque for a small amount of money. And I really do mean small: it was maybe £20 at most. This was not a grant but an emergency loan that would then be paid back in increments from our weekly, already insufficient, benefits, thus plunging us further into the same poverty cycle.

Reading Kayleigh Garthwaite's *Hunger Inc.* triggered a core memory related to hunger and food aid, such as the abject shame on my mum's face as she begged them not to give her food vouchers: 'These children will go hungry if you try and give me vouchers. I won't use them.' My mum, intensely proud and private to the point of paranoia, couldn't stand the idea of handing over the stigmatising vouchers in public, in a small town.

I tell this story because in reading *Hunger Inc.* it angered me, although it didn't surprise, how little has changed despite the rise and rise of very visible food aid and the proliferation of food banks in particular. In those intervening decades, the false narrative that hunger and poverty are an individual's fault is still prevalent and that charity but without dignity still exists. Back then there were no food banks, but I do recall a truck going round one of our council estates giving out huge, sweaty slabs of cheese, blocks of butter and cans simply marked 'Stewed Steak', which we were led to believe was from EU 'food mountains', and which my mum called 'mystery meat' and, chiming again with the interviewees in the book, 'Someone else's rubbish', sensibly refusing to eat it.

Call it food poverty or insecurity or, my preference, 'food violence'. Call it a permacrisis, a hunger industrial complex, food apartheid – but don't call it an 'emergency' because, if it is, then, as one food aid worker states in this book it is, 'a 40-year emergency'. While the world's wealthiest countries have been entrenching 'emergency' charitable responses as a solution to a systemic problem, as Kayleigh so rightly says, 'the current charitable food aid system does not work. If it did, we wouldn't see yearly skyrocketing rates of food insecurity across countries that are some of the wealthiest in the world.'

Of course, as my story – just one of many describing a childhood of food poverty and financial precarity – illuminates, food insecurity is just one cog in a whole complex machine of systemic privation. And so much outlined in Kayleigh's research informed me and helped me reframe my own experiences, both as a former beneficiary of food aid and an invested member of the public. The concept of a legal right to food; solidarity, not charity; trauma-informed and healing-centred approaches to food aid; a 'cash first' policy; mutual aid and food sovereignty. I did not know these terms, but this book gave me the privilege and gift of naming my feelings about food poverty.

In the following chapters you will find examples of organisations not only leading by innovation but doing so successfully. This book creates a discourse that enables us to learn from their ethos, their triumphs and challenges while also analysing current iterations of food aid and their limitations.

This research is truly an invaluable primer for those seeking to understand food insecurity, those wishing to make a lasting impact on it from the frontline, and indeed, those like myself who have experienced food insecurity and want to know how to move forward with hope, to support those in the same situation now.

Introduction

Live mice.
Dashboard cleaning spray.
Starbucks Nespresso capsules.
A jar of organic eggnog-flavoured cashew cream.
A rotten turkey.
Russian Petushok cockerel shaped sugar lollipops.
Bone broth.
Snack biscuits for hamsters.
Liquid smoke.
Birthday cake candles (but only for 18th and 50th birthdays).

These are just a few of the bizarre items I've seen turn up in food bank donation boxes and warehouses during my two and a half years of research into charitable and community food aid across the United States, Canada, the UK, and other 'rich-but-unequal' countries in western Europe.[1]

Food banks have become the most visible face of poverty in wealthy societies. But can food charity really solve the problem of hunger?

Since 2019, the number of food banks in the UK has outnumbered McDonald's outlets by nearly two to one. Austerity measures, amplified by a continual erosion of the social security system, have led to 'emergency' charitable food aid provision in the form of food banks, food pantries, and related forms of food provision becoming an increasingly expected part of daily life. The Covid-19 pandemic exacerbated the need for charitable food support, forcing many people to seek assistance from food banks for the first time. This shift brought urgent attention to the pervasive issues of food insecurity and hunger on a global scale. Outraged headlines told us that teachers, nurses, and middle-class graduates were now using food banks.[2] Termed 'the newly hungry',[3] there was a renewed spotlight on food bank use due to middle-income

1

families seeking support as a result of the financial pressures of the pandemic. Seen as more deserving than previous food bank visitors, these newly hungry typically had mortgages and cars, and were often self-employed or business owners.

It's important to point out how the terms 'food bank' and 'food pantry' differ significantly across geographical contexts. In the UK, typically a food bank directly provides emergency food parcels to people in crisis, usually through a referral system, with pre-packed parcels designed to meet short-term needs. By contrast, in North America and other countries across western Europe, a food bank tends to function as a centralised warehouse that distributes food to front-line agencies such as food pantries (which can operate in a similar way to a food bank in the UK context), rather than directly to individuals. The concept of a food pantry also varies – in the UK, it often refers to community-based initiatives providing affordable food, usually through a membership model, to promote sustainable food access and reduce waste. Meanwhile, in North America in particular, a food pantry serves as the primary point of emergency food distribution to individuals and families, often offering a client-choice model where people can select the food items they need.

Today, charitable food aid continues to be framed as an *emergency* response to hunger. But what kind of emergency lasts for decades? 'Emergency' suggests that this is a situation that will pass. But the subsequent cost-of-living crisis, political instability and worsened global food insecurity have resulted in governments and the private sector increasing 'emergency' food aid initiatives, while the structural causes of food insecurity and poverty have been left untreated. Corporate involvement in food charity soared during the pandemic. Businesses ramped up donations, while increasing their control and improving their public image. This allowed big companies and organisations to take control of food aid in the UK and around the world, making temporary, charity-based food support seem like a long-term fix – even though it's not a real solution – in some of the world's wealthiest countries.

This introductory chapter explains why we need to be concerned about the continued growth of charitable food aid, including issues of precarity, dignity, corporate power, and human rights. Through meeting those who are working and volunteering in food banks and food pantries, and running anti-poverty, anti-hunger and community organisations, alongside internationally acclaimed scholars and researchers working at the forefront of critical debates on food insecurity and poverty, *Hunger, Inc.: Building Solidarity Beyond the Food Bank* brings together a narrative that shows just how embedded charitable food aid is across wealthy societies, and how it is often misrepresented as a false solution to hunger and poverty.

Reimagining spaces of charitable food aid reveals a central contradiction at the heart of contemporary responses to hunger: should we focus on making food banks more dignified, efficient and expansive, or should we be working to end the need for them altogether? This book asks whether it's possible to do both. Can we improve the immediate experience of people accessing charitable food aid, while simultaneously challenging the systemic conditions that make food aid necessary in the first place? Food banks and charitable food aid are not solutions to hunger – they are symptoms of a system that produces scarcity amid abundance. This book insists on a radical rethinking: one that refuses to normalise so-called emergency relief as a permanent fixture and instead demands a future where food justice, rights and solidarity replace food charity.

FOOD CHARITY DOESN'T SOLVE FOOD INSECURITY

The current charitable food aid system is fundamentally flawed. If it worked, we wouldn't see the persistent, growing rates of food insecurity in some of the wealthiest countries in the world. In the UK, one in seven people are struggling in a category of deep poverty that Trussell calls 'hunger and hardship',[4] where individuals have little or no savings and likely carry significant debts.[5] *Guardian* journalist Patrick Butler explains that Trussell developed this term in response to the 2024 Labour Party manifesto, which promised an 'end to mass dependence on emergency food parcels'. For those experiencing hunger and hardship, it's not just about food; they struggle to afford energy bills, clothing and other basics. A financial crisis, such as job loss or an unexpected large bill, can send people towards charitable food aid.

Similar patterns are evident across North America: 13.5 per cent of US households were food insecure at some time during 2023,[6] meaning a staggering 18 million people had difficulty providing enough food for their household because of a lack of resources. This is the highest rate of food insecurity ever experienced in the US. In Canada, the proportion of the population experiencing food insecurity is even higher, with 16.9 per cent of Canadians classed as food insecure in 2022. Overall, the proportion of individuals in households experiencing food insecurity has increased by 5.3 percentage points from 2018 to 2022.[7]

The current model of food banking is widely accepted to have originated in the US before spreading to neighbouring Canada, steadily advancing across Europe and other parts of the globe. But the roots of food charity itself stretch back far earlier. Soup kitchens, church-based relief, and other forms of charitable food provision have long served as a moral and material response to poverty, particularly during moments of economic crisis or social unrest. From Victorian workhouses to Depression-era breadlines, the distribution of food to people living in poverty has often been used to manage, moralise and contain poverty, rather than eliminate it. Academics Andrew Williams and Jon May point out that much of the way food banks in the UK operate today – such as using referral vouchers, handing out pre-packed food parcels, relying on corporate sponsorship and organising food drives – is rooted in specific historical developments.[8] These operational practices, along with the narratives about who is deserving of help and concerns about fostering dependency, emerged from particular political tensions and moments of social conflict.

The current dominant 'emergency' charitable food aid system has become entrenched in many rich-but-unequal countries due to a combination of economic, social and political factors that reflect deep structural inequalities. Despite being wealthy, many developed countries have significant income inequality, leaving large portions of the population vulnerable to food insecurity. Inadequate and insecure wages, underemployment and precarious work have left many people unable to meet their most basic needs. This disparity has increased the need for charitable food aid, which is intended to function as a temporary safety net for people who fall through the cracks of social protections.

At the same time, many wealthy nations have reduced public spending on welfare and social safety nets due to austerity measures or political ideologies.[9] Addressing food insecurity through charity can then be seen as politically expedient because it allows governments to avoid tackling deeper systemic issues, such as poverty, wage inequality and the need for affordable housing or healthcare. By continuing to rely on – and even celebrating – a charitable food aid model, political leaders can express concern for people experiencing poverty without committing to the types of redistributive policies or social protections that would effectively combat poverty and inequality.

Charitable and community organisations then have little choice but to step in to fill the gap. Food banks, pantries, food clubs, social supermarkets and related forms of community food support originally intended to provide short-term crisis relief have progressively become long-term, corporate-backed solutions to chronic food insecurity and poverty. Surplus food has increasingly been redirected to charitable food aid through partnerships with corporations and supermarkets, reinforcing the false perspective that this represents a 'win-win' solution to the separate issues of food waste and poverty. This model, which benefits corporate interests by framing food donations as social responsibility initiatives and offering tax incentives, masks broader issues that lead to overproduction and surplus food in the first place.

The reliance on food banks and other forms of food aid has also become gradually more visible and normalised in many rich-but-unequal countries. It's hard to visit a supermarket without seeing a food bank donation point. Paying for groceries at the self-checkout, you're often asked to round up your bill to donate to your local food bank. Instagram adverts urge donations to food banks. TV and radio adverts do the same. Entering the workplace, there might be a food bank collection going on there, too, especially at Christmas time. In the UK, even just 10 or 15 years ago, this wasn't the case. Food banking was starting to become more visible back then, but now it has become an everyday expectation.

It will likely be easier to turn the tide on this institutionalisation in the UK than in countries such as the US and Canada, which have a much longer and established history of charitable food aid.

But as we'll see throughout this book, the growing momentum around advocating for alternatives based on solidarity and rights, not charity, in rich-but-unequal countries shows that there *is* another way forward.

RESEARCHING CHARITABLE FOOD AID
IN RICH-BUT-UNEQUAL COUNTRIES

I started researching charitable food aid in 2013 when food banks were becoming increasingly visible in the UK. There was outrage at headlines announcing one million food parcels had been given out by Trussell. I spent almost seven years volunteering at and visiting a Trussell food bank in Stockton-on-Tees, north east England – first as a researcher and volunteer, then as a friend and occasional helper. During that time, I met hundreds of people who shared their experiences of using a food bank with me.[10] I wrote about the stigma and shame so often attached to using a food bank, as well as how health inequalities can interact with accessing charitable food. From my perspective as a volunteer, I was able to gain a better understanding of the dynamics, conditions and challenges of charitable food aid. Concluding my 2016 book *Hunger Pains: Life Inside Foodbank Britain*, I warned against the continued institutionalisation of food banking and the structural issues – namely poverty and inequality – that would need to be addressed in order to tackle rising numbers of people seeking emergency food aid.

Since then, the continued growth of food banks and rise in corporate partnerships with companies such as Tesco, Asda and Amazon has led me to look to North America as a comparison. Learning from countries with a much longer history of charitable food aid than the UK, such as the US and Canada, led me to co-found the Global Solidarity Alliance for Food, Health, and Social Justice (GSA) in 2018.[11] The GSA is made up of non-governmental organisations (NGOs), national networks, grassroots activists and academics, mostly based in North America and western Europe. As a collective, we argue that it's crucial that emergency provision is not framed as the solution to increasing food insecurity across our rich-but-unequal countries. We know that emergency food provision is not addressing the root causes of poverty and is neither a dignified nor long-term solution. Leaving the matter to charity exacerbates poverty by allowing governments and citizens to consider the problem solved, while ignoring income policies and human rights.

Since forming, we've focused on collective actions, including open letters, a podcast series, international briefing papers and monthly virtual gatherings, strengthening a diverse, growing network of right to food and nutrition advocates. One key aim has been to elevate the voices of those working on national and local anti-hunger advocacy in international policy fora, such as the Food and Agriculture Organization (FAO) and United Nations (UN) Special Rapporteurs. At the same time, we recognise the tensions between pursuing a rights-based approach and one based on solidarity. Rights-based approaches focus on legal frameworks and institutional change but can be slow, bureaucratic and top down. Meanwhile, solidarity emphasises immediate mutual aid and horizontal community action but may lack the resources and infrastructure to create lasting structural change. This book documents the ongoing network building of our collective amid these tensions, capturing a precarious, ever-worsening situation of food insecurity and growth in charitable food aid use.

In October 2020, during the pandemic, I received funding to begin research for this book. At the time, I had no idea if I'd actually be able to visit the people and organisations I'd been building relationships with through the GSA network since 2018. Would I have to rely on Zoom calls instead of seeing their work on the ground in the US, Canada and countries in Western Europe? After several waves of the pandemic, I finally made my first trip to Heidelberg, Germany in May 2022, where I spent a week with global human rights organisation FIAN International. Over the following two and a half years, I visited more than 90 organisations in six countries – Canada, the US, the UK, Italy, Belgium and the Basque region – across 24 cities and numerous small towns. Across all of these places, the political ideologies, historical contexts and relationships between the state and civil society play a crucial role in shaping how charitable food aid is organised and implemented. These places were chosen because they each represent different welfare regimes, policy environments and histories of charitable food assistance, allowing me to answer my central research question of how food charity has become institutionalised and corporatised in diverse contexts.

Despite their different welfare systems, food banks and charitable food aid have expanded rapidly across these places in recent years. In countries such as the US, UK and Canada, decades of cuts to public services and social security have pushed more people to rely on charity to meet basic needs. In parts of Europe where welfare states were once stronger, rising inequality and permacrises have led to societies responding to hunger not through universal rights or strong social security systems but through charity, which is often presented as a generous, temporary fix. But food charity is neither neutral nor short term. It has become deeply institutionalised, with major corporations, including supermarkets and food manufacturers, playing a central role. These companies donate surplus food, support food charities and benefit from tax breaks and positive PR, all while continuing to profit from the same economic systems that produce food insecurity in the first place.

My research followed a patchwork ethnography approach, characterised by short-term field visits and the use of fragmentary, yet rigorous, data.[12] This flexible and creative method allowed me to move between places and perspectives, studying how people and organisations respond to food insecurity across different contexts. Many of my field sites were chosen through pre-existing relationships with front-line NGOs and scholar-activists connected to the GSA network. I set out to learn directly from those developing innovative responses to poverty and food insecurity – both inside and outside the charitable sector, including grassroots initiatives offering alternatives to traditional food aid. Over 18 weeks in the field, I spent more than 300 hours as both a researcher and volunteer in food banks, pantries, urban farms, community kitchens, solidarity emporiums, food co-ops, farmers markets, food policy councils and mutual aid groups. This resulted in over 55,000 words of field notes, capturing observations, conversations and reflections in real time.

My ethnographic approach involved 'patching' together short-term research visits, online and in-person semi-structured interviews, ethnographic field notes, participant observation, meeting and event notes, volunteer ethnography and email correspondence, and analysing documents including annual reports. I immersed myself in communities, often for several weeks at a time, to understand how charitable food aid was attempting to meet people's basic needs. I was interested in how individuals and groups accessed, produced, distributed and consumed food, revealing not only cultural norms and practices but also deep-seated and wide-ranging inequalities that varied according to gender, race, place, social class and disability.

We ate together. Sitting on long tables alongside farm workers, I had the best mozzarella I've eaten in my life in a social co-operative farm on the outskirts of Rome. We drove around cities to huge warehouses full to the brim with surplus and donated food. We travelled into rural parts of the US where there was no grocery stores for miles but always a food pantry. I walked for miles, rode the bus, subways and metro, and occasionally took a taxi or Uber, keen to get a feel for the city I was in.

Visiting organisations in person allowed me to learn so much more than I would have had I just met volunteers and workers online. I ate a delicious three-course meal made from surplus food on tables decorated with starched white linen tablecloths with vases of beautiful yellow flowers as part of a community meal in the Tenderloin neighbourhood in San Francisco, California, an area notorious for destitution, homelessness and substance abuse. I spent a morning listening to music, eating with and being inspired by a group of grassroots activists in the Forst area of Brussels who distributed surplus organic food in efforts to ensure people achieved the right to good quality, healthy food. I saw some of the worst poverty and destitution I've ever seen in my life in the Downtown Eastside neighbourhood of Vancouver, with people laid face down on the concrete sidewalk, bodies contorted by what I later learned was likely the ravaging effects of fentanyl. I visited so many huge food bank warehouses that after a while they all started to blur into one, although the immense scale and logistics of what I was seeing never failed to shock me.

Sometimes the idea of food security and a right to food seemed like a fantasy when faced with the ingrained poverty and destitution I was seeing. This made me even more aware of my own right to food, as I sought out the best places to drink speciality coffee, eat locally sourced food and drink craft beer. As a white, cisgender woman who would be considered middle class, I knew that my identity shaped how I was seen and treated in the spaces I entered. I was given access and trust in ways that others – especially people from more marginalised backgrounds – might not have been.

I was also careful not to further burden those working and volunteering in communities. I tried my best to ensure my visits weren't extractive and offered to volunteer or share resources. My research was shaped by a feminist politics of care – one that values listening closely, understanding people in context and paying attention to power in relationships. Throughout the research, I kept a daily journal to reflect critically on how my presence, privileges and assumptions were influencing what I was seeing, hearing and understanding. This immersive ethnographic approach allowed me to explore and document power dynamics, identifying how these can impact peoples' access to food, as well as witness how relationships in charitable food aid spaces can be fraught with implicit rules and expectations. Alongside ethnographic field visits across North America and Europe, throughout this book I share stories about my own involvement in volunteering, offering a snapshot of the volunteer experience.

My visits to organisations and neighbourhoods across my fieldwork were often guided by researchers and grassroots activists who I'd already formed relationships with through GSA. I was therefore lucky to have a ready-made network of support – at the end of the day, we could reflect on what we'd collectively seen, heard and experienced. In cities where I didn't have that, such as Vancouver or San Francisco, I would find myself feeling overwhelmed as I attempted to study food insecurity and a right to food amid destitution the likes of which I had never seen before. Across the San Francisco Bay in Deep East Oakland, I saw fresh bullets wedged into the wooden frame of a now defunct town fridge at Homies Empowerment that was collateral damage from a drive-by shooting just a few hours before. Diego Rodriguez, caretaker of research and development, told us that they'd noticed the fridge wasn't cooling as it normally would, and when they had a look, they saw the bullets. All of the food inside was spoiled. 'We are here intentionally in the community. This is the reality we face', Diego told me. At least five people came looking for the fridge when we were standing there and left disappointed. The community response to the fridge being damaged showed the solidarity that Homies were fostering in their East Oakland neighbourhood. A couple of months after my visit, I saw on their Instagram page that a brand new, double-fronted fridge had been bought following community donations. The hashtag #SolidarityNotCharity was tagged with the photograph of Diego beaming next to the fridge, showing how this was a shared effort, built on mutual respect and support, not charity.

Taxi drivers relentlessly asked why I was asking them to drop me off in 'dangerous neighbourhoods', with one driver in San Francisco insisting I show him the address of where I was going before he would even think about letting let me out of the car. 'You see that?' he asked me, pointing to the car's rear window, which was taped up with thick black tape. 'Every time I get it fixed it gets smashed again with people trying to steal stuff.' As we drove through the Tenderloin streets, past street encampments and a heavy police presence, he locked the doors so people couldn't try to get in at the stop lights. As we pulled up to the building where I was headed for a community dinner at food justice non-profit Farming Hope, he asked, 'Are you sure you want me to drop you off *here*?' I got my phone out to show him the Google Maps location and he obligingly unlocked the doors.

At the time of my visit in May 2023, San Francisco was home to 37 billionaires, including Mark Zuckerberg, CEO of Meta, and Brian Chesky, CEO of Airbnb. Excluding Elon Musk, 21 of the wealthiest people in the world reside in the San Francisco Bay Area, their aggregate net worth totalling a staggering $867 billion.[13] Yet more than 3,000 people were living unsheltered on the streets or in tents.[14] Persistent homelessness and an unbelievably high cost of living had turned downtown San Francisco into a bit of a ghost town. Big businesses were moving out, like Nordstrom and Whole Foods. 'This city is not in a good place', was something I heard

11

from taxi drivers, volunteers and people I chatted to on the bus. 'The city is dying.'

I felt completely worn out by the sheer scale of the neglect and desolation in Vancouver. Walking back after a day of visits, I would quicken my pace and feel a huge wave of relief when I finally returned to the hotel. My jaw ached constantly from the tension carried in my body. Although it's known as a city of best practices for sustainability, liveability and quality of life,[15] the Downtown Eastside remains one of the poorest neighbourhoods in the whole of Canada,[16] known for its high crime rates, blatant drug use, unemployment and housing issues. The area is home to the largest number of single-room occupancy hotels (SROs) in Canada, where I heard accounts of appalling living conditions – rats scurrying through rooms, cockroaches crawling over everything and filth everywhere. Meanwhile, I was staying in a four-star hotel in the old stock exchange building, where uniformed porters opened the door for me every day. The hotel was just a couple of minutes' walk from the Downtown Eastside Oppenheimer District, an area with a high concentration of housing and social services, including East Hastings Street where many of the homeless encampments could be found. A few weeks before I arrived in Vancouver, the city did a clean-up of the area, removing 80 or so tents from the streets' 100-block area. Seraphina Skands, from Queen's University, explains the area like this: 'In this area, the seemingly mundane act of walking in public is complicated by the things and activities we presume to be "private", drug use, sleeping, and even dying, take place on sidewalks, down alleyways, and in parks.'[17]

Yet at the same time, the Downtown Eastside community is also known for radical grassroots activism, Ian Marcuse from Vancouver Neighbourhood Food Networks (VNFN) told me. The VNFN is a network of community organisations committed to promoting food security in neighbourhoods across the City of Vancouver. The Downtown Eastside Neighbourhood House (DTESNH) is part of the network, and aims to offer a dignified and welcoming space for all community members. DTESNH also runs a right to food zine which promotes the human right to healthy, nutritious, affordable food, presented with dignity.

Downtown Eastside is also an area of rapid gentrification, which I experienced first hand. I felt a deep sense of guilt walking past Vancouver's multiple homeless encampments, stepping over broken glass, used needles, discarded metal spoons and human shit as I made my way to a local café to pay CAD$6 for a flat white. The privilege of me visiting cities such as New York, San Francisco and Vancouver was something I never took for granted. Growing up in an old mining village in one of the most deprived areas of County Durham, I could never have imagined travelling around the world to work. In all of my visits, I was guided by a feminist ethics of care framework that sought to understand, listen and contextualise what I was seeing.

The hundreds of hours and thousands of miles I travelled during 2022 and 2024 confirmed to me that charitable food aid is not, and can never be, the answer to hunger and poverty. It's precarious and relies on donations of surplus food and financial contributions from corporations and the general public. The food offered might not be culturally relevant, despite workers' and volunteers' best efforts. This is important, as we know that people from Black and minority ethnic populations are disproportionately accessing charitable food.[18] The food might not be especially nutritious or even very appealing, such as the eggnog-flavoured cashew cream I saw lingering on a shelf in a community supermarket in Seattle, or the liquid smoke in a not-for-profit grocery market in Vancouver. Yet seeing first hand the tireless efforts of those on the front lines of charitable food aid – especially their push for alternative models – helped me understand the power of collective strategies of resistance and imagine a future where food charity is no longer necessary.

HOW THE BOOK UNFOLDS

This book is divided into two parts. Part I diagnoses the systemic problems inherent in charitable food aid, highlighting its limitations and the ways it can perpetuate and worsen existing inequalities. Part II offers alternatives and solutions based on solidarity and human rights, advocating for a shift away from charity and towards sustainable, justice-driven approaches to food insecurity.

Chapter 1 traces the history of charitable food aid, examining its evolution from a temporary emergency measure to an entrenched part of welfare systems in rich-but-unequal countries. It explores the rise of food banks and how they became institutionalised, as well as the broader social, political and economic forces that have shaped the development of food charity, particularly within the context of ongoing global crises or 'permacrisis'. It explains how the international growth of charitable food aid has also been encouraged by legislation incentivising the charitable donation of surplus food from corporations.

Chapter 2 explores the complexities and contradictions in using surplus food in charitable food provision, problematising the idea of offering leftover food and products to 'left behind people', as academic Graham Riches has warned.[19] A deeply problematic feature of the corporate-based charitable food aid model is the joining up of two separate issues that require different solutions: food waste and hunger.

Chapter 3 outlines the impact of viewing food insecurity as an 'emergency' to be addressed through short-term charity rather than systemic change. It also outlines why we need to reframe 'emergency' charitable food amid the permacrisis context we are living through globally. This chapter also explores the significant public health implications of relying on charitable food aid during times of crisis.

Running charitable food aid spaces requires enormous levels of care and commitment. Chapter 4 draws on the experiences of front-line workers and volunteers – whose voices are often unheard – to emphasise the skill and persistence involved in negotiating complex relationships with donors, charities and beneficiaries. At the same time, it focuses on the tensions that many working on the front line feel – how opportunities for pursuing alternative approaches based on social justice have been threatened by recurrent crises, reducing the time and energy available to advocate for change.

Chapter 5 argues that the right to food should be seen as a fundamental human right rather than a charitable gift. It explores how the right to food is one of the most violated in the world and emphasises the importance of enshrining it in law to ensure that all people have access to nutritious and culturally appropriate food. The chapter advocates for a shift from charity to rights-based approaches to addressing food insecurity, while also acknowledging the need for solidarity-based approaches that focus on horizontality and mutuality.

Chapter 6 presents alternatives to charitable food models, based on dignity and reducing stigma, drawn from my field visits to food banks, food co-ops and community organisations in the US, Canada and western Europe. It explores urban farms, community kitchens and solidarity emporiums as ways to provide healthy, nutritious food and work towards food justice for all.

Concrete policy proposals to move beyond charity and address the root causes of food insecurity are the focus of Chapter 7. It presents a 'call to action', urging policymakers, corporations, activists and communities to push for policy change, narrative change and solidarity-based approaches to food justice.

The final substantive chapter, Chapter 8, highlights the power of solidarity in resisting corporate-backed charitable food aid. It examines how grassroots organisations and collective action can drive systemic change by challenging and reimagining the dominant charity-based model.

Finally, the Conclusion reaffirms the book's central argument: food charity, despite good intentions, fails to address the root causes of food insecurity and deepens structural inequalities. It issues a clear call for long-term, systemic transformation: a shift from corporate-backed charity models to rights-based, solidarity-driven approaches that confront poverty and hunger at their source. Real change demands collective action – and a bold reimagining of a system where access to adequate food and a liveable income are guaranteed for all.

WHAT THIS BOOK AIMS TO DO

How do you feel when you walk past the food bank donation box in the supermarket? Does it shock you that we are in this situation? Or – be honest – do you not even notice it anymore?

Charitable food aid has become celebrated, criticised and nor-malised all at once. Members of the public who generously donate to charitable food aid are branded 'heroes'. Corporations who support food banks are applauded for their corporate social responsibility. People who access charitable food aid are told by politicians that they need more education – to budget better, to learn how to cook, to stop spending money on cigarettes and mobile phones. But what really drives the need for charitable food aid is poverty and inequality.

The spread of corporate-backed food charity across high-income countries offers a stark warning, one this book amplifies. As this model extends its reach, it signals not progress but a con-tinued erosion of human rights, with governments stepping back from their obligations as duty bearers. The hundreds of hours of observations, meetings, shared meals, conversations and inter-views I conducted gave me a first-hand understanding of how corporate-backed food charity is failing to meet people's basic needs, despite the huge amount of care and labour from those on the front lines who are dedicated to offering charitable food aid.

Charitable food aid must be radically rethought. In wealthy yet profoundly unequal societies, and far beyond the so-called Global North, we must resist the global export of a broken system. This cannot be left to individual acts of goodwill. It demands solidar-ity – between those experiencing hunger, those resisting inequality and all who refuse to accept that dignity can be rationed out by charity.

Changing the conversation is essential. Imagine if every single donor who donated a tin of food to a food charity wrote to their local politician to protest against insufficient social security policies? Or if food aid workers and volunteers went on strike? Together with political advocacy, harnessing the public goodwill around charitable food aid could be an incredibly powerful tool in ending the need for charitable food altogether.

In the face of overlapping crises, we have an opportunity to reject charity as a substitute for rights, and to build a future rooted in solidarity, where access to nutritious food is not an act of gener-osity but a guarantee.

PART I

The Problems of
Charitable Food Aid

1
The Past and Present of Charitable Food Aid

St. Mary's Food Bank was established in 1967 in Phoenix, Arizona. Founded by John van Hengel, 'the father of food banking', the idea for what is often declared to be the world's first food bank came from his time receiving food from a local soup kitchen after finding himself divorced and homeless. While waiting in line for food, he encountered a mother who was collecting food for herself and her ten children from the dumpsters behind a grocery store. Van Hengel approached the bins and discovered frozen food that was still safe to eat, as well as loose carrots and some stale bread. 'The woman had healthy kids who obviously didn't eat bad at all', he said in an interview with *The Los Angeles Times* in 1992. The woman suggested there should be a place where food could be stored for people to pick up rather than being thrown away. According to the St. Mary's Food Bank website, on hearing her story 'van Hengel's heart was broken'.[1] He took a vow of poverty and became a devout Catholic. And so, the first food bank was born.

Named a 'food bank' due to its transactional nature (and apparently named by the woman van Hengel met), the concept was based on the premise that individuals and companies with excess food could 'deposit' it, and those in need could 'withdraw' it. As St. Mary's grew, they accepted anything and everything in terms of donations – 10,000 live chickens, 500 cases of anchovies, one million marshmallow Easter bunnies. 'We figured if people were kind enough to donate food, we would find a place for it', van Hengel said. Van Hengel's food bank didn't distribute food directly to people who were experiencing hunger but worked through a network of decentralised distribution centres such as food pantries and community centres.

The concept proved to be a popular one. Van Hengel then went on to become the founder of several other food banks across the country, leading to the development of the national organisation America's Second Harvest in 1979 (which later became the organisation Feeding America, the nation's leading domestic hunger relief charity). In 2023, there was even an illustrated children's book published about van Hengel's life, which urged children to reflect: 'If John could do this, what can we do?'

The US food-banking model reached Canada in the early 1980s as a response to the economic recession the country was experiencing. In 1981, the Edmonton Food Bank was established in Edmonton, Alberta. Just as in the US, food banks quickly became seen as a go-to response to the twin issues of hunger and food waste. Initially intended as a short-term solution, food banks quickly became a permanent feature of the social security safety net, growing rapidly as government support for social welfare programmes declined. Writing in 1986, academic Graham Riches argued in his prescient first book that the rise of food banks in Canada was not only concrete evidence of the collapse of the social safety net but that it also posed many questions about the role of food waste in capitalist societies.[2]

Just a few years later, food banks made their way to Europe. Sister Cécile Bigot heard about the concept through Francis Lopez, founder of the Edmonton Food Bank in Canada, and set up France's first food bank in Paris in July 1984 with the ethos, '*L'aide alimentaire, porte d'entrée vers l'inclusion*', which translates as, 'Food aid, a gateway to inclusion'. Apparently, the first two donations were from a French company donating bread every day and another donating fish – 'How could we not see that as a symbol from on high to continue growing this food bank?'[3] Like the American and Canadian food banks, the first European food bank was religiously motivated.

This was shortly followed by the first Belgian food bank in Brussels, after which the European Federation of Food Banks (FEBA) was launched in September 1986 to provide a single organised body that would represent food banks at a European level. Today, FEBA is a growing network of 351 food banks active in 30 European countries. Food banks were established in Spain, Italy, Ireland and Portugal by 1992. Between 1994 and 2001, food banks were established in Greece, Luxembourg and Poland.

The UK did not set up food banks until several years later. In 2004, the Salisbury Foodbank was set up in a garden shed and garage by Trussell, a charity founded on Christian principles and now the UK's largest food bank franchise. Food banks started to become much more widespread post-2010, with Trussell starting to publish data on food bank usage from 2011. In 2023–4, Trussell distributed parcels from 1,711 locations across the UK.[4] But figures from Trussell alone cannot fully explain the scale of food bank use. The Independent Food Aid Network (IFAN)[5] has identified at least 1,172 independent food banks.[6] There are also thousands more food banks run by the Salvation Army, hospitals, schools and universities. William Baker and colleagues at the University of Bristol found more than 4,000 school-based food banks in primary and secondary schools across England,[7] which equates to one in every five schools running one. In addition, there are thousands of community food projects, including food pantries, social supermarkets and soup kitchens, the majority of which fall into the category of 'charitable food aid' provision, relying on volunteer labour, charitable grants and surplus food. According to data collated by the Food Standards Agency (FSA) Food and You survey in England and Wales, however, most adults reporting food insecurity do not access a food bank or a social supermarket.[8] For example, in one wave of the survey, 4% of respondents had used a food bank in the past year, and 94% had not. Similarly, 5% had used a social supermarket, while 79% had not.

The growth and institutionalisation of the dominant emergency food-banking model is well illustrated by the reach and influence of the Global FoodBanking Network (GFN), a spinoff organisation from Feeding America in Chicago and existing food banks in Canada, Argentina and Mexico, which was established in 2006. Across six continents, in nearly 50 countries, GFN member food banks serve a staggering 39 million people. Funded by some of the most powerful food corporations in the world, including Kellogg's and PepsiCo, the GFN is focused on further anchoring corporate charity as a global strategy to feed people living in poverty through the repurposing of waste from industrial food processes. Their intent, according to its 2023–6 strategic plan, is to 'expand the presence and influence of food banks all over the world'.[9] GFN have also been repositioning themselves as drivers of high-level climate action, claiming that 'the food banking model is uniquely positioned to address food waste and climate change'.

A GFN member, the Mexican FoodBanking Network (BAMX), became the first organisation in the world to earn carbon credits for rescuing surplus food. BAMX earns these credits by diverting surplus food from landfills, where it would emit methane, a potent greenhouse gas. Marrying up the redistribution of surplus food with efforts to reduce climate change is equally as problematic as suggesting surplus food solves poverty. This framing overlooks the root causes of food overproduction and waste, focusing on managing symptoms without challenging the broader systems driving both hunger and environmental degradation. Yet as journalist Chris Costanzo, founder of *Food Bank News*, has written: 'Monetization of food waste is the latest innovation in the rapidly growing voluntary carbon market.'[10] Food banks can then effectively greenwash climate change by presenting their efforts to reduce food waste as a comprehensive climate solution, while diverting attention from the systemic environmental harms caused by corporate-backed industrial food systems. Food banks are thus operating within a 'permacrisis' context, where ongoing crises – economic, social and environmental – overlap and exacerbate one another.

A 'PERMACRISIS' CONTEXT

Permacrisis: an extended period of instability and insecurity, especially one resulting from a series of catastrophic events.

The *Collins Dictionary* word of the year for 2022 was 'permacrisis', reflecting the continuation of crises we have witnessed since the onset of the Covid-19 pandemic. The pandemic exacerbated the acceleration of charitable food aid and led to dramatic increases in food insecurity in the Global North, particularly for people in marginalised communities, reflecting an intersectionality of experiences shaped by race, disability, social class and gender.

The temporary support put in place was shown to be effective at relieving food insecurity. In the US, for instance, the Census Bureau's Supplemental Poverty Measure estimates that in 2020, 2.9 million people were lifted out of poverty due to the Supplementary Nutrition Assistance Program (SNAP), along with 300,000 children by the school lunch programme. All recipients were given at least an additional $95 per month in benefits,[11] with Black and Latinx households benefiting most from the additional SNAP allocations. Visiting organisations in the US, I witnessed the anxiety the end of the assistance was creating for workers and volunteers on the front line. Would the help be extended? What would be in its place? If the government could help during the pandemic, why not now when need continued to grow? These measures came to an end on 1 March 2023 in the US, leaving organisations seeking ways to make up for the gaping hole in people's resources.

In the UK, we saw a similar story regarding how cash-based support could work. In March 2020, the government announced an uplift to Universal Credit and Working Tax Credits worth £20 a week in response to the pandemic. Initially planned to last for one year, the policy was extended by six months in the March 2021 budget. In July 2021, the government confirmed that it would not be extended further. Research by the Institute for Fiscal Studies shows that the emergency programme of a £20 increase to Universal Credit led to a sharp fall in the number of households living in absolute poverty during the 18 months it was in force.[12] But the uplift was not experienced evenly, with disabled people on legacy benefits such as Employment and Support Allowance excluded.

For the first time, the UK government offered a grant of up to £100,000 to those running a front-line food aid charity in England,[13] with the Department of Environment and Rural Affairs (DEFRA) directly funding and supporting the provision of emergency food aid. FareShare, the UK's national network of charitable food redistributors, received direct financial support from DEFRA to supply non-perishable food to community food organisations, which 'undeniably expanded and entrenched charitable food aid as essential welfare provision', according to academic and author Maddy Power.[14] However, it is important to note that neither Trussell nor IFAN directly accepted government funding to purchase food for distribution through their networks.

Temporary support was also widespread in Canada and across European countries. Between April 2020 and December 2021, the government of Canada committed an unprecedented CAD\$330 million towards the Emergency Food Security Fund to support emergency food providers and charitable food organisations, including food banks and meal programmes. In the province of British Columbia, a CAD\$3 million emergency grant was announced in March 2020 to 'buy and distribute food, pay employees and cover other costs essential to the delivery of their food programs'.[15]

Academic Daniel Warshawsky from Wright State University in the US has noted how the pandemic highlighted the 'structural weaknesses and the fragility of the charity-based emergency food system'.[16] In particular, many European food banks faced higher costs, lower food stocks, uneven food donations and lower numbers of volunteers and personnel as demand for food relief increased sharply. The ongoing cost-of-living crisis placed further demands on charitable food, with food banks having to ration the food given out due to shortages in donations, and in some cases having to turn people away.[17]

Since the pandemic, the level of need has continued to grow. Food banks are increasingly purchasing food to keep up with the demand, as well as extending their opening hours as more and more people in employment are seeking a food parcel. One in five people being referred to food banks are from a working household.[18] There is a greater need for kettle boxes and cold food packs that people don't have to heat up. Donations are dropping. Consequently, food banks are directly buying food to stock the shelves, increasing the time and labour involved in ensuring food parcels are available. In September 2023, I interviewed Sabine Goodwin, director of IFAN, the UK's network of independent food aid providers, to see how food banks were coping. Sabine told me:

The situation is getting increasingly more fragile and worrying. And from our perspective it was very difficult to report on this because you keep saying things can't get any worse. And actually they do. So how do you say that? How do you get that message out there in a way that is clear, compelling and believable? It's no exaggeration to say that this winter coming up is likely to be the worst that has been seen for many, many years. But because we've said that last year, that seems unbelievable. But it's not. So we just have to be consistent and keep saying, 'This is the reality'.

In the UK, Trussell released their mid-years stats in November 2024, which showed more than 1.4 million emergency food parcels were distributed to people experiencing hardship between 1 April and 30 September 2024. This is 69 per cent higher than the same period five years ago.[19] Families with children were most affected, with 63 per cent of parcels going to households with children under the age of 16. To give some context, in 2012–13, when I first started researching food bank use, just over one million parcels were given out in the whole year by Trussell. As people are not just receiving food parcels from Trussell, this only gives a partial view of the scale of food bank use.

From April to July 2023, every independent food bank responding to IFAN's survey reported that they had supported people who previously had never visited a food bank. Surplus supplies have also dwindled, and 45 per cent of IFAN member organisations surveyed in November 2023 reported receiving poor quality food that is not fit to be distributed. Food disposal is then added to their growing lists of tasks, which are often unpaid.

In considering the relationship between charitable food use and food insecurity, food assistance is not always a direct result of hunger alone. While food insecurity is undeniably a key factor in the decision to seek out food aid, other elements such as social exclusion, a lack of access to services and the stigma surrounding food assistance can play an equally important role. It's also crucial to acknowledge that not all individuals who experience food insecurity rely on food banks. In fact, food banks are just the tip of the iceberg when it comes to understanding the complexities of hunger, food insecurity and the broader issue of a right to food. Many food insecure people never access food assistance for a variety of reasons, including social barriers or a lack of awareness about available services. In the UK, for instance, 86 per cent of households experiencing food insecurity never even access a food bank, according to the Department of Work and Pensions Family Resources Survey published in March 2024.[20] For those that do, the support received is often temporary, insufficient and partial. The food given out can be unsuitable for certain health conditions, inedible or past its use-by date. There may also be cultural and socio-economic barriers that prevent people from accessing and consuming the types of food being donated. Recognising this broader context is vital for fully understanding the scope of food insecurity and the limitations of charitable food aid as a solution.

As charitable food aid use continues to increase, so too does food insecurity and associated ill health. NHS figures published in January 2025 showed that hospital admissions due to lack of vitamins are soaring in England, with iron and vitamin B deficiencies becoming increasingly common.[21] Almost 11,000 people in England were reportedly hospitalised with malnutrition in 2022.[22] Doctors have warned that the cost-of-living crisis has led to a rise in Victorian illnesses such as scurvy and rickets, with cases quadrupling since 2007–8. The Joseph Rowntree Foundation's 'Destitution in the UK' report revealed that approximately 3.8 million people experienced destitution in 2022, including around one million children.[23] This is almost two and a half times the number of people in 2017 and nearly triple the number of children. Putting that 3.8 million figure into context, it is a couple of hundred thousand short of the entire population of Croatia.

Doctors are increasingly prescribing non-medical essentials such as food, fuel and financial advice in pilot projects in the UK.[24] Given the NHS is already at breaking point, though, is social prescribing the answer to poverty? In the US, 'food is medicine' is a growing trend, referring to programmes that integrate nutritious food into healthcare to address diet-related diseases, often involving food charity organisations. The number of people living in food insecure households in the US in 2023 increased to 47 million, including 13 million children, according to a report by the US Department of Agriculture (USDA) – the highest rates ever recorded. In 2023, more than 50 million people accessed the Feeding America network of food banks,[25] which saw them distributing more than 5.3 billion meals to people experiencing hunger. While these programmes can improve health outcomes, they risk becoming yet another temporary solution if they fail to address systemic issues such as poverty, inequality and access to affordable, healthy food.

This burgeoning need and worsening situation has resulted in a search for alternatives. Former Prime Minister Gordon Brown has introduced a new concept to the emergency food aid space in the UK: the 'multibank'. According to Brown, the multibank model is both an anti-poverty and anti-pollution project. Working with corporate giant Amazon, Brown states that 150,000 families in need have received 1.5 million essential goods for free. The multibank encourages 'businesses and hard-pressed householders to embrace the circular economy' through the creation of a repository 'bank' of surplus but reusable household goods, food, clothes, toiletries, furnishings, bedding, children and baby goods.[26] It is claimed that the Fife Big House project 'has thus unlocked a method to tackle two of Scotland's biggest challenges at the same time – waste and family household poverty'.

Yet in the same week that Brown urged the development of a 'coalition of compassion' to support the nationwide expansion of the multibank initiative, hundreds of Amazon workers went on strike in the UK, Europe and the US to protest against their dire working conditions – stringent targets, low pay and ongoing precarity. Amazon driver Jessie Moreno, striking in California, said: 'It's the living conditions, it's respect, and of course it's money. We're living in poverty conditions while the CEO, Jeff Bezos, gets richer and richer off our hard work, and we're just struggling to put food on the table.'[27]

The irony of Amazon being the main supporter of the multibank initiative while failing to protect its own workers from poverty cannot be ignored. Amazon are also contributing to ever-growing inequality in the UK. Despite making a £222 million profit, Amazon's main UK division paid no corporation tax in 2022 – the second year in a row that this part of Amazon paid no corporation tax in the UK.[28]

Continually rising levels of food insecurity, 'solutions' designed to simultaneously reduce waste and tackle poverty, and growing corporate interest in charitable food aid create a perfect storm by perpetuating a cycle where systemic issues go unaddressed. Corporate-driven 'solutions' often prioritise redistributing surplus food rather than tackling root causes such as poverty or inequitable food systems. This approach normalises dependence on charity, frames waste as inevitable and allows corporations to greenwash their practices, reinforcing broken systems instead of fostering sustainable change. In our 'permacrisis' context, it is clear that we cannot food bank our way out of poverty and food insecurity.

I want to close this chapter with what reads, in retrospect, like a warning from the so-called father of food banking, John van Hengel. In his obituary in the *New York Times* in 2005, van Hengel reportedly reflected on the explosive growth of food banking by saying: 'We're feeding millions, and it's not costing anyone anything. But it scares me to look back because I just had no idea it would grow into this.'[29]

2

Food Surplus and the Growth of the Hunger Industrial Complex

Rescued food. Food waste. Surplus food. Unsold food. Whatever we choose to call it, there is an increasing perception that the joining up of two distinct issues – surplus food and food insecurity – can be a 'win-win' solution to the growing need seen in the UK and other rich countries in the Global North.

It's easy to see why the two are linked. Surplus food can be abundant and of amazing quality. Many organisations are reliant on it to ensure people can access food at all. But surplus food can also arrive spoiled, or worse. Volunteers in both Rome and Vancouver told me of donations arriving full of live mice. Being inundated with particular foods can mean giving out Christmas confectionery in April, which is hardly dignified. Charitable food aid organisations also face precarity in terms of the amount, type and suitability of food received. Many workers and volunteers in front-line organisations work relentlessly to redistribute surplus food to people facing food insecurity, but a growing number are realising this is not a long-term solution to either food waste or food poverty.

Before exploring some of the complexities and contradictions of redistributing surplus food in emergency and community food aid settings, it's important to consider what we mean by 'surplus food' and try to understand the scale of the problem. Simply put, surplus food occurs when the supply of food exceeds demand for it. There are many reasons this can happen, encompassing every stage of the farm to fridge to fork process. In November 2023, Kris Gibbon-Walsh, then chief operating officer at FareShare, the UK's 'largest charity fighting hunger and food waste', told me:

If you look at the supply chain, it's about 30 million tonnes of food wasted total. About half of that's edible, about six million. Half of that's in our houses, as consumers. But actually, the next biggest proportion is in the farms, there's about three million tonnes in farms and loads of that is edible. So the most edible food is actually in the farms, you've got less than in manufacturing, and you've got even less in retail and even less in the stores themselves. And then you got some in hospitality. So the reality is that when you look at the total value, and then what's redistributed, farms are a massive source.

The most common reasons for food wasted at industry level are overproduction, damaged packaging, manufacturing or order mistakes, stock control issues, cosmetic standards and confusion surrounding dates (best before, use by, display until). As Kris explains, it could be something as simple as a new product that didn't quite work out:

Sometimes the charity will get plant-based turkey products, which are a new line and they didn't quite work, and that's why it became surplus. But things become surplus for all kinds of reasons. They become surplus because the label's got the wrong shade of grey on it, or because the allergen labelling's wrong, or because they overordered, or because suddenly it's sunnier than they expected it to be and they need more barbecue stuff so a line gets rejected from 3,000 stores and there's nowhere for it to go.

There is also the link to climate change and environmental justice. One of the most oft-repeated statements I've read when researching food waste is, 'if food waste were a country, it would be the world's third largest emitter of greenhouse gas after China and the USA'. According to climate action NGO the Waste and Resources Action Programme, globally 25–30 per cent of total food produced is lost or wasted, and food waste is estimated by the Intergovernmental Panel on Climate Change to contribute 8–10 per cent of total human-caused greenhouse gas emissions.[1] Nearly 40 per cent of all food grown annually in the US goes unsold or uneaten.[2]

The joining up of charitable food aid, surplus and the environment is fast becoming a popular one. For the GFN, '[f]ood banks are a win-win solution for people and the planet and can help to mitigate the impacts of climate change'. They are 'an unsung hero of climate action'.[3] Research from 2019 by members of the world's three largest food bank networks – FEBA, Feeding America and the GFN – found the networks recovered 3.75 million metric tons of food, enough to fill nearly 1,292 Olympic swimming pools, preventing over 12 billion kilograms of greenhouse gases from entering the atmosphere via food decomposition.[4]

Embedded within these figures and declarations is the idea that as a society we have a moral imperative to distribute this food to people who are hungry – where else should it go? Surely, if people are queuing up at food banks around the world, it's better for this surplus food to end up on their plates that in the bin, isn't it? This seemingly persuasive narrative can be hard to dispel. A high-profile example of this narrative in action is King Charles' Coronation Food Project in the UK. Launched in November 2023 for the king's 75th birthday, the project aims to help those in need, while at the same time reducing the amount of surplus food being thrown away. Speaking in the *Big Issue*,[5] the king said: 'If a way could be found to bridge the gap between them, then it would address two problems in one.' Headlines boasted of the ways the king reduced his own personal food waste, suggesting that he 'eats daily slices from the same cake until it's finished as part of a drive to curb his personal food waste'.[6] Are the monarchy really best placed to solve the UK's poverty crisis? After all, the king's coronation just a few months earlier had cost the taxpayer a staggering £72 million,[7] at a time of ever-increasing inflation and destitution.

Following the announcement, Sabine Goodwin, director of IFAN, wrote in the *Big Issue*: 'It certainly suits supermarkets to redirect surplus but, in reality, poor quality food often ends up at food banks where volunteers add waste disposal to their endless list of tasks.'[8] Despite well-meaning efforts, trying to connect food poverty and food waste then risks exacerbating these issues rather than resolving them. A report by environmental campaign group Feedback found that 91 per cent of food aid workers are forced to discard food donations from businesses, due to them being damaged or inedible;[9] 85 per cent of food aid workers reported feeling frustrated, angry or sad when receiving unusable food donations.

Charity FareShare, 'the proud partner' of the king's campaign, has long campaigned for the UK government and industry to invest millions of pounds towards tackling food waste. In February 2024, it was announced that the UK government would introduce a £15 million fund to help farmers redistribute surplus food.[10] The fund was promised again in December 2024 following a high-profile campaign.[11] Conservative MPs backed FareShare's campaign, yet Tory policies are a key reason why so many people are facing food insecurity in the first place. The idea of using surplus food to feed hungry people is clearly a popular one with the general public, too. Over 114,000 people signed a petition calling for funding for FareShare, while 88 per cent of the public believe surplus food should be donated.[12] After all, 'Where should the food go if it doesn't go in the bin?', as Kris Gibbon-Walsh, then COO of FareShare, asked me when I interviewed him in November 2023.

I was on the receiving end of food that should not have ended up on people's plates while visiting West Virginia in October 2022. Josh Lohnes, director of the Food Justice Lab at the Center for Resilient Communities, West Virginia University, said there was a congregate feeding programme called Manna Meal that offers breakfast in Charleston. He'd been before, pre-Covid, and said we could have breakfast and a chat with the volunteers to see who was using it and why. The breakfast programme was located inside St. John's Episcopal Church in the heart of Charleston and serves as many as 400 people a day, 365 days a year. Checking out their website the night before our visit, it told me they offered 'well-balanced, nutritious meals'.

We arrived just after opening time at 8 am and as soon as we walked in I felt deeply uncomfortable. Most of the people coming for food were struggling with ill health and were likely homeless, looking at the huge backpacks and overflowing carrier bags they had with them. We were so out of place that I felt mortified. There were stacks of white polystyrene containers laid out on some tables at the front of the church hall. We each collected one, and Josh picked up a carton of still-frozen orange juice. Opening the lid of the container I discovered a pale yellow circle thing I was told was egg, two ultra processed hot dog-type sausages, a dry-looking sugary cinnamon bun and a freezing cold overripe banana. I ate the egg-type thing but couldn't face the sausages. After one bite of the bun I started to feel nauseous. The overpowering heat in the stuffy church was overwhelming. I felt guilty for wasting food that should have gone to people who were there because they were hungry, but mostly I felt sick that people were being fed such poor quality food in the first place.

As we were eating, a guy sat down with us and we got chatting. He told us he was homeless and came to Manna Meal as it was one of the only places he could find food and warmth in the morning. 'The food is bad but at least it's something', he told us as he steadily ate everything in his container. Just before 9 am the volunteers came round and told us we needed to get moving. As we stepped outside, we watched the Feeding America truck unloading more donated food from corporate retail giant Walmart, one of Feeding America's largest donors.

Academics and NGOs have long warned of the dangers of conflating food waste distribution with food insecurity reduction. Evidence shows that surplus food has not prevented food insecurity and hunger.[13] For example, in the US and Canada, countries with a much longer history of using food surplus in charitable food provision, it tells us quite clearly that feeding surplus food to people on a low income is ineffective, inequitable and an affront to human dignity.[14] While the expansion of organised surplus food redistribution might at first glance *seem* like a win-win solution, the practice fails to reduce food waste levels while undermining policies designed to address food insecurity. Surplus food can be inedible or past its best and include random items that are frankly useless (remember the liquid smoke I mentioned earlier?). Often, those working tirelessly in front-line and grassroots organisations have to expend time and effort redistributing these products to other organisations who might (or might not) be able to make use of them.

This is the paradox in the food surplus as hunger relief relationship. Although there are millions of metric tons of food available (which is the issue), the charitable system leads to food aid organisations facing a situation of both excess and scarcity. During times of excess, charities become inundated and inadvertently function as de facto waste disposal services. In times of scarcity, they are compelled to deny assistance or manage distributions in ways that can contradict their core values. Donating surpluses is a way for companies to receive lucrative tax incentives and be seen to fulfil their corporate social responsibility duties, while simultaneously relieving themselves of surplus products that are often not fit for purpose, or at the very least not suitable for a healthy and fulfilling diet. I witnessed first hand the tensions that need to be navigated between those running charities and the donating corporations. Refusing donations was often seen as unthinkable – if that happened, maybe the company would stop donating altogether? Added to that was the guilt of workers and volunteers about not wasting items they'd been given.

FOOD SURPLUS LEGISLATION

One proposed 'solution' to ensure surplus food ends up being fed to hungry people and not used as animal feed is the introduction of legislation at city, state and country level. In 2016, France became the first country in the world to pass a national law specifically against food waste, establishing mandatory partnerships for donations.[15] The law, referred to as *Loi Garot* after the National Assembly member who submitted the law proposal, requires supermarkets to donate unsold food to charities and food banks. It also includes measures to raise public awareness about food waste and encourages food donations from businesses. Food waste expert Marie Mourad has explained how the policy earned significant international attention, having been inaccurately portrayed as a complete 'ban' on food waste:

> The idea that the law made donations 'mandatory', the provision which gained the most attention is only partly true. The regulation mandates that supermarkets above 400 square metres sign an agreement with food assistance organisations to donate their excess edible, unsold products. Yet, the obligation to sign a contract obligates neither that supermarkets donate a minimum quantity of their unsold products nor give at regular intervals.

As such, a supermarket could theoretically comply by donating one box of chocolates per year.[16]

In practice, this legislation can actually cause further labour for those working in charitable food aid spaces. As Kris Gibbon-Walsh, chief operating officer of FareShare in the UK, told me:

> The French Food Bank, the last time I was there a couple of years ago, they were saying it's [the legislation] made their lives hell because they were already getting loads of food from loads of their partners. But then they became a dump, because the law meant that the organisations had to donate it. And they were like, 'Well, you have to take everything' and then they would just have to take rubbish, and therefore they had to have loads more volunteers having to deal with everything and it made it much worse rather than much better.

Such food waste legislation is becoming increasingly popular across rich-but-unequal countries. Following the French example, other states and cities across the US and Europe are taking inspiration and creating their own surplus laws. Since 2022, California's Senate Bill 1383 has mandated that certain food businesses donate as much unused edible food as possible to food recovery organisations, and requires all grocery stores in the state to participate in the food recovery programme.[17] Specifically, it aims for California to recover at least 20 per cent of edible food that would otherwise be discarded. In May 2023, I visited the California Association of Food Banks in downtown Oakland to find out more.

California produces nearly half of the nation's fruits and vegetables, yet more than one in five Californians – about 8.4 million – currently struggle with food insecurity. Because of vast structural inequalities,[18] much greater levels of hunger are experienced by Black, Latinx and Hispanic people. Black Californians are more than twice as likely to experience food insecurity than white Californians. Lauren Lathan Reid, director of communications and member engagement, told me that the new law phases food donors in under two tiers. SB1383 requires Tier 1 businesses (large grocery stores, wholesalers) to donate surplus packaged food and Tier 2 businesses (restaurants, hotels, schools) to donate prepared food to food recovery organisations, reducing food waste and methane emissions. 'Every one of the food banks are doing something different on SB1383', Lauren told me. At the time of our meeting, it was voluntary for food banks to participate. From January 2024, the second tier of being required to donate would be implemented, which includes restaurants and their surplus. 'How can we distribute trays of lasagne?' Lauren asked. Participating food banks will also need to keep accurate monthly records or risk potential fines. Reflecting on the French food waste laws, then General Secretary of FEBA Angela Frigo told me:

> Another disadvantage that we notice is that it was, in France, it was kind of shifting the problem of food waste from the supermarkets to the food banks or the charities because then the risk is that the supermarkets are afraid of getting a fine or a sanction. So, they are donating good food, but they are also donating as much as possible. So, then the risk is that the food bank or the charity is receiving good food but also bad food. And then it means that the food bank or the charity has to deal with the disposal of this food. So, you are just, if you want, shifting the problem from one stage to another one on the food supply chain.

The role of corporations has been further encouraged by legislation incentivising the charitable donation of surplus food. In Italy, the *Legga Gadda* (Gadda Law) allows city municipalities to implement tax deductions on food donations made towards charities,[19] while a recently implemented law in Spain will see food waste essentially disappear from official measurements of surplus, as it is instead distributed to families (but only those with children) on a low income via the use of shopping cards.[20]

Under these laws, charitable food aid providers and food banks become part of a mandated waste disposal system rather than poverty alleviation agencies. This shift risks further normalising food charity as a permanent fixture, distracting from broader systemic solutions such as living wages, stronger welfare policies and the right to food. While the legislation might tackle methane emissions, it does little to challenge the overproduction and economic structures that create both food waste and hunger in the first place. A more just approach would prioritise preventing surplus food at the source and guaranteeing food security through rights-based policies, rather than relying on redistribution as an afterthought to corporate excess.

THE 'HUNGER INDUSTRIAL COMPLEX'

Have you ever thought about why big companies are vocal supporters of charitable food aid through food banks and food pantries? Supermarkets such as Asda, Sainsbury's and Morrisons in the UK, along with Walmart in the US and Loblaws in Canada, claim to be fighting hunger in their communities. Multi-billion dollar corporations such as Amazon engage in delivering food and surplus items to charities across the globe. What's in it for them?

The role of corporate philanthropy in supporting and maintaining charitable food aid is an underdiscussed topic in the UK, but it deserves far greater attention. In North America, highly paid company executives and managers are often on the board of charitable food organisations, shaping decisions and benefiting from tax and financial incentives to donate. Companies then benefit from a 'halo effect' that aligns with their corporate social responsibilities, while charities gratefully receive the donations. Writing in a North American context, long-time community activist and author Andy Fisher describes how a self-perpetuating 'hunger industrial complex' is a central part of the charitable food system. Andy told me:

Almost every corporation in America is donating money to food banks because it makes them seem charitable. It gives them a veneer of responsibility, and it bolsters their corporate reputation. As a result, you have these food banks which are supposedly addressing food insecurity, and maybe even addressing poverty in some cases, that are tied into corporate America, into the food industry in particular. And you have the board members, many of whom are tied into corporate America. They're avoiding policy decisions or policy advocacy, decisions that would be controversial, that would raise the cost of doing business for these corporations, especially the minimum wage. You see very few food banks who are willing to step into that minimum wage space or into anything what I call beyond the nutrition safety zone, getting into immigration policy or tax or housing or transportation policy.

When we look at the tax incentives, the avoidance of waste disposal fees and the positive publicity in being positioned as hunger fighters, Andy argues, 'there are few incentives to actually seek to end hunger, as it would be bad for business on all levels'.

I remember reading Andy's book, *Big Hunger*, on the train ride back home from Birmingham not long after I started working there in 2017. Much of what Andy was writing about resonated with what was happening in the UK. Although there are completely different welfare states in the US and the UK, reading *Big Hunger* made me interested to explore how we in the UK could avoid ending up in the institutionalised, corporate-backed charity landscape we see flourishing in North America. Trussell had been calling for 'a food bank in every town', and was forming partnerships with Tesco and Asda worth tens of millions. These involved establishing food bank donation points in every supermarket, which also contributed to the companies' profits. At the same time, these supermarkets were in the headlines for not paying a real Living Wage, with Asda staff reported to be using food banks themselves.[21] In fact, employees of Sainsbury's, Asda and Amazon have all reported using food banks, despite their employers being frequent donors to charitable food aid. These companies have been criticised for not providing their workers with a real living wage or adequate employment rights, yet ironically, they are some of the most vocal supporters of the 'emergency' food aid system.

I asked Andy to tell me more about what had changed in the hunger industrial complex since he wrote *Big Hunger*, which predates the pandemic and global food security crisis. He said the sheer amount of money that became available to front-line organisations – either directly from governments or from philanthropy – had changed the charitable food aid landscape:

Everybody was writing their $200 checks. So they're [food banks] just more entrenched and more institutionalised. You see them buying bigger buildings. You see them buying second warehouses. I mean, there's just this growth curve that's gone on. You see their budgets have increased substantially almost across the board. So they're serving more and more people with more and more food, and they're buying more food, too, which is just a whole other weird thing that happens. It really subverts the food waste argument. They've developed all these secondary markets.

There are obviously many differences as well as similarities between North America and Europe – too many to describe here. Different (sometimes absent) social security safety nets. Desperate housing crises. Wholly inadequate wages. Varying political contexts. But what is visible across all of these countries is the growing presence and role of big corporations in response to food insecurity, which makes possible the further retreat of the state.

'ONE STEP BEFORE THE GARBAGE'

A clear example of the power dynamics between corporations and anti-hunger organisations can be seen in my visit to the Banco Alimentare del Lazio in Rome in March 2023. Italy's first food bank was founded in 1989 by the Fondazione Banco Alimentare Onlus (FBAO) to collect and redistribute food surpluses to charitable organisations. Today, FBAO operates a network of 21 food banks across Italy, including the Banco Alimentare del Lazio. Researchers from the Food Poverty Observatory in Rome arranged for us to visit the food bank on a Friday morning. To give an idea of scale, in 2022, the Lazio food bank distributed approximately 7,000 tonnes of food to around 110,000 people, collaborating with 450 non-profit organisations.[22] All of this is achieved with just eight paid staff and 15–20 volunteers working Monday to Friday from 6.30 am. The 1,600 square metre warehouse – the largest in the region – opened in 2021. It costs half a million euros per year to run the organisation.

Staff member Marco* made us an espresso with a proper coffee machine, which was a first for me in a food bank! When I said as much they told me that the pods they use are part of the donations they're given from a big company that sends regular donations, but they aren't suitable to give out to people across the 450 organisations they're working with. After all, how many people living in poverty have access to a Nespresso machine at home? The food comes from surplus in agricultural production, the food industry,[23] large-scale distribution and organised catering, public institutions and food outlets.

Food also comes from the Fund for European Aid to the Most Deprived (FEAD), a European Union (EU) fund that provides food, material support and vouchers to help reduce poverty in EU countries. Staff and volunteers at the food bank must weigh and account for everything supplied by FEAD and records must be kept for ten years. As we walked around the warehouse, I was shocked to see that the FEAD products, including tins of minestrone soup and bags of rice, were emblazoned with labels bearing the EU flag, alongside the FEAD logo and a warning in large capital letters that this was a '*Prodotto non commerciabile*', or non-marketable product. There is an inherent challenge to someone's dignity in being given food that is branded as 'non-marketable'. When I visited the then general secretary of FEBA, Angela Frigo, in Brussels in October 2023, I asked her why FEAD products were branded in this way. Surely it was highly stigmatising and inappropriate? Angela told me:

> In some countries like Italy, Belgium or Poland, there's the EU flag, while in other countries there's no flag. There's nothing. There's no reference … In some countries they prefer that the food is easily recognisable to avoid that this food could go to the black market or a second market that could be sold again.

At the Alfa Felix Solidarity Emporium in Guidonia, around 40 minutes' drive from the centre of Rome, I saw the branded FEAD tins again. I was told the food was specially produced this way for two reasons: first, for food safety; and second, for communications

* Names throughout this example have been changed to protect anonymity.

– the EU want to know how much of the food is being given out, so FEAD food must be tracked separately. There were two separate tills at the solidarity emporium for this purpose.

Back in the warehouse, crate after crate of orange-flavoured San Pellegrino sparkling water and Coca-Cola with lemon were piled up next to a glut of tins of beef in jelly. A massive 25 per cent of donations to the food bank are soft drinks, Marco said. There's a peeling sticker on the front of the walk-in refrigerator saying Coca-Cola had paid for it. Marco took us to another part of the warehouse, an area he called 'the saddest part'. There were huge, battered cardboard boxes lined up next to one another, full to the brim of, for want of a better word, 'stuff'. Starbucks Nespresso pods, dented boxes of Christmas panettone,[24] and dashboard cleaning spray (a whole tray full) were piled on top of organic toiletries and hamster treat biscuits (another first for me). Marco told us that donation boxes with live mice stowed inside have found their way to the warehouse after people donated items without thinking about the consequences of putting a fresh turkey in a donation bin. 'We are just the step before the garbage', he said, shaking his head sadly.

During the course of the four hours we spent being shown around every part of the warehouse, it became clear just how much effort and organisation is needed to manage corporate donations while adhering to the values of their organisation. Every three months the food bank must send a document to corporate donors so they can get their promised tax discount under the *Legga Gadda* law. Marco told us how volunteers spend time and effort sorting through the donated items to create a presentable parcel that can be handed out to organisations, stressing the need for dignity and respect.

I asked what they could do about surplus arriving in this way, and Marco told us that volunteers from the company donating it were invited to come and sort through what had been sent. They would then come and promise to do it better next time. It was clear Marco was unhappy at the way it worked, but there was also a tension around the fact the organisation didn't want me and the other researchers to specifically name the companies donating the surplus, as they were worried the companies might stop sending products, despite their inadequacies. The particular company sending the boxes of stuff are happy to say they give so many kilograms of donations, but they wouldn't want the photos I was taking of the messy boxes of donations to be made public. Writing in a US context, Andy Fisher explains: 'Donors want free waste removal, convenience, a tax deduction, and the halo effect that accompanies hunger relief efforts. Donors do not want to be judged about the quality of the food they provide. Food bankers fear that if they decline a product the donor will not deliver other desirable items.'[25]

All of this navigating and negotiating requires time, effort and tact. 'Everything we do is based on relationships', Marco stressed. Relationships with people in the 450 plus organisations across the region, with the large donor companies and with their volunteers. The food bank describes itself as 'a very complex organisation'. Every day the organisation needs to adapt the work it does depending on who is there to volunteer. Sometimes the younger volunteers will stay for just a few weeks, while the older volunteers sometimes struggle to operate the Excel spreadsheets necessary to track the food coming in and out of the warehouse.

Everything I heard during that visit underlined just how tricky it is for charities – both the workers and volunteers – to navigate the institutional tensions and power dynamics involved in dealing with powerful companies. 'It's complicated', Marco told us. 'Relationships are important, as is trust.' I asked if they have ever refused donations. 'We can't act in this way', Marco said. In fact, they've only refused once, 'a crate of amaro,[26] the first ever donation to the food bank!' As we stood chatting towards the end of the visit, a large Italian pasta company arrived with a donation. Marco explained that sometimes the drivers are late, as the food bank is always last in line for donations – again, the phrase 'one step before the garbage' was repeated. But he continued, 'It's always about the relationship. It costs companies to bring us their waste. It costs their time, their effort. Charity is not free.'

The tensions in trying to keep donors happy, ensuring there's enough food to meet people's needs and having enough volunteers to sort that food are a daily struggle for Marco and his colleagues. Power dynamics play out at every turn. But what happens if food banks and pantries were to say, 'Enough is enough'?

CORPORATE SOCIAL (IR)RESPONSIBILITY?

The West Side Campaign Against Hunger (WSCAH) in New York City pioneered the first customer choice pantry model in the US over 30 years ago, offering fresh fruits, vegetables, whole grains, proteins and dairy. WSCAH has been running since 1979, operating out of the Church of St. Paul and St. Andrew on West 86th Street on the Upper West Side. It was a gorgeous bright late October day in 2022 when I arrived. Executive Director and CEO Chef Greg Silverman was outside the church as people picked up their bags of food bursting with fresh fruit and vegetables from the desks set up on the sidewalk.

Greg took me on a tour of what used to be WSCAH's sit-in pantry, which since the pandemic had become a place where food was organised into bags to be handed out to the customers waiting outside. Greg said that WSCAH created the customer choice pantry model as part of a wider mission aimed at ensuring all New Yorkers had dignified access to a choice of healthy food and supportive services. People accessing the food pantry are first of all screened for benefits to make sure they're getting everything they're entitled to, such as SNAP, or food stamps, and Free or Reduced School Meals. When people receive their food, 52 per cent of what's given out in the parcel is fresh produce and is intended to provide five days' worth of food for people and their families, once a month.

Greg refuses to accept unhealthy food, such as soda, hamburger helper (a box of dried pasta with seasoning that is designed to be cooked with ground beef) and rice-a-roni (a boxed food mix that consists of rice, vermicelli pasta and seasonings). His stance is somewhat controversial, as these products represent the companies that are making the donations. Greg explained the reasoning behind the refusal:

After about six months running WSCAH in the summer of 2017, I was told by a WSCAH staff member that I would be unhappy with the contents of the day's food donation from one of the local food banks. I went out to view the day's in-kind food deliveries and found 10 pallets of high-salt, pre-packaged rice and pasta meals, high-sugar sweetened beverages, and high-fat/salt/

sugar snack foods. Were we supposed to serve this mountain of salt, sugar, and fat to our customers?

We internally discussed the delivery items and decided as a team, we absolutely would not distribute these unhealthy products to our customers. The products did not fit into any of our healthy eating food categories, were not culturally relevant snack foods, and were outside the bounds of any nutritional guidelines we adhered to. I promptly got on the phone and asked the donor to pick up the truckload of thousands of pounds of processed junk. Seemed like a simple ask of a business partner. The reaction was less than cordial, and thus my real learning in the emergency feeding sector began.[27]

Once Greg had navigated the institutional politics of refusing tonnes of junk food, WSCAH found that their food distribution went from 20 per cent fresh produce to 52 per cent fresh produce. Their website makes a clear statement on their values around nutrition to potential donors to avoid any doubt:

We do not accept or distribute highly processed, high-salt, or high-sugar foods, including sugary cereals, most canned soups, and boxed or canned prepared foods, such as macaroni and cheese, meat stews, or beefaroni-like products. We also do not accept or distribute expired or damaged foods.

DO: Give generously. Give foods you would serve to your family.

DON'T: Give anything expired, open, or damaged. Give something you wouldn't eat.

The differences concerning corporate power in both the Lazio Food Bank and WSCAH are clear to see. Food banks and anti-hunger organisations can become dumping grounds for surplus items that are unsuitable, inadequate and unhealthy. Due to the complex relationships that must be maintained, it can be difficult – if not impossible – for charities to say 'no' to surplus. The companies that donate are praised for their corporate social responsibility efforts, and in turn they celebrate those working and volunteering on the front lines who are doing the daily work of redistributing often unsuitable surplus food.

In the UK, the Morrisons supermarket chain has partnered with both Trussell and FareShare. They've run campaigns such as 'Ask for Ellen', which allowed customers to get two free crumpets with butter and jam in their cafes in the school holidays, trying to remove the stigma of saying 'I need help'. In their supermarkets, you can purchase 'pickup packs': green paper bags filled with items for the local food bank or community group with labels such as 'holiday hunger' and 'tinned meals' written in felt tip marker on the front. But at the same time, Morrisons are taking over local corner shops in often isolated and deprived rural villages or council estates and charging hugely inflated prices. According to research by the UK's consumer champion *Which?* in 2023,[28] essential budget range items are hardly ever stocked in these smaller Morrisons shops, even though two-thirds of people earning under £21,000 shop there at least once a week. They found that shopping in a Morrisons Daily cost 21 per cent more compared to shopping in their larger branches, the biggest price differential across all the supermarkets.[29]

Journalist Adam Bychawski has termed Coca-Cola a 'corporate scrooge' in response to their boasting about Christmas donations in 2022.[30] Bychawski states that Coca-Cola, the world's richest beverage company, announced that it would donate the equivalent of a meal to charity for every person who visits its Christmas truck tour in the UK. However, the end of the announcement explained Coca-Cola would in fact give a maximum of just £25,000 to the charity FareShare. In real terms, this amounts to less than 0.01 per cent of the £259.9 million profit Coca-Cola made in the UK – the equivalent of a millionaire donating three £30 turkeys to charity, notes Bychawski. By contrast, Coca-Cola handed out £440 million in dividends to shareholders in 2021, dipping into its reserves to do so.

Similar criticisms can be made when looking at multi-billion dollar company Amazon, owned by the second richest person in the world, Jeff Bezos. Since 2020, Amazon's charitable programmes have contributed more than €350 million in donations across Europe.[31] I often saw food pantries in the US that featured Amazon wish lists on their websites that donors could purchase from. Yet, as touched on earlier, it is frequently reported that their workers are forced to work in precarious, unsafe conditions. In 2021 in the US, for example, Amazon warehouses had a rate of 7.7 injuries per 100 workers, compared with 4 injuries for every 100 workers at all other warehouses.[32] Staff in the UK, US and Europe are often on strike over tax, market abuse and workers' rights.[33] Some Amazon staff have alleged that even their toilet breaks can be timed.[34] Rachel Fagan, GMB Union organiser, said workers at the Amazon warehouse in Coventry were demanding better pay but also considered performance targets to be unfair. She said: 'In the middle of winter, people are dressed like they are going to the gym, with T-shirts, shorts and trainers, because of the physical work. It's really hard work and it has a toll.'[35]

Not only do corporations benefit in terms of shedding their surplus and receiving tax incentives, they are also positioned as 'changemakers', 'nurturers' and 'catalysts'. These are just some of the descriptions of donors that I saw proudly displayed on the walls of the Daily Bread Food Bank and engraved into concrete paving slabs outside Second Harvest, the largest food rescue in Canada, while I was visiting Toronto in May 2024. Visiting both organisations, I was struck by the prominent displays listing donors by the size of their financial support. At Second Harvest, the two donors who had contributed over CAD$1 million were labelled as 'Seeding the Future'. The 'Pollinators Circle' represented those who had given more than CAD$250,000. Uber Eats was in the 'Grower's Circle', with a donation of over CAD$100,000. The celebratory nature of these relationships masks the often poor working conditions of corporations that fail to pay or promote a living wage or who oppose unionisation efforts.

With this in mind, we must consider whether Amazon is the best company to partner with former UK Prime Minister Gordon Brown in his 'multibanks' initiative. Yes, Amazon's charitable efforts are significant, including their response to the earthquake and wildfires in Türkiye, the donation of 160,000 nappies to the Tafel food bank in Berlin and the delivery of over 400 pallets of toys from Hasbro to Ukrainian children through their humanitarian aid hub in Poland. But the aforementioned concerns surrounding Amazon's working practices and the contradiction of their charitable giving with their tax practices need to be brought into focus.

Food surplus has become the backbone of food banks – and the justification for a growing system of corporate-led charity. Big companies such as Amazon donate leftover food and products and are celebrated for doing so. Surplus food exists because the system is built to overproduce, exploit workers and prioritise profit over need. These corporations benefit from the same economic conditions that create hunger in the first place, and then offer leftovers as charity. This lets them clean up their image, get tax breaks and avoid any real accountability, all while keeping the system exactly as it is. And it shapes how we think about hunger – not as a political failure but as something to be 'solved' through donations and good intentions. We need to stop asking how to make food charity more efficient and start asking why we live in a society with so much waste and so much poverty – and who benefits from that contradiction.

RUNNING ON EMPTY:
WHERE HAS ALL THE SURPLUS GONE?

Many organisations told me that surplus supplies have been dwindling. While reducing overproduction in the first place is obviously essential, a lack of surplus has meant increased competition between charitable organisations, highlighting the precarity and sustainability of relying on food sourced in this way. In January 2024, George Wright, then CEO of FareShare, said:

There's too much competitive behaviour amongst the charities, when they should be working to make better use of their collective resources … America is three times more efficient than the UK when it comes to food redistribution … The current competitive regime in the UK is less efficient and can result in volume being moved from one type of charity to another – that's a really bad outcome for the end beneficiaries.[36]

But should the UK be looking to the US for inspiration, given that in the latter the distribution of surplus food via emergency food aid is utterly entrenched, yet hunger and food insecurity continues to rise?

Charities must continually adjust to evolving supply chains in the private sector, rather than vice versa. I was frequently told that organisations were having to seek out new ways to ensure a steady, adequate food supply. In February 2024, I asked Andrew Forsey, director of Feeding Britain, a charity network working to eliminate hunger and destitution in the UK, how as a network they were responding to this challenge. Andrew described how they were working towards a 'virtuous circle' of supply and demand:

> I was rather pleased as a citizen to see that the supermarkets were finding ways of preventing so much food becoming surplus in the first place. But of course that then meant less food was becoming available for community food projects. And then, because so many people who used to donate food are now struggling themselves, there was less food being donated. So I thought, 'Right, it's really incumbent upon us given those two new developments to rapidly diversify our supply of food, and ideally have the bedrock of our supply come from non-surplus sources'. So local wholesalers, local manufacturers, local producers, and increasingly now we started to broker some national deals, some of the wholesalers, suppliers, and manufacturers so that anything that then came through from surplus or donations was a bit of a bonus rather than the core element of our supply chain.

Meanwhile, Sabine Goodwin, director of IFAN in the UK, told me:

> What's becoming clear is just how ineffective a response it is, which is what we've been saying for a long time. So we all know that conflating the problem of too much food waste and poverty is never going to result in a solution or reduction in either. So it's just so important that we keep talking about that, especially when we're talking about food pantries, because food pantries are starting up all over the place, and they haven't got the surplus food, because it's just that there isn't enough of it.

Visiting their head office on the outskirts of Brussels in October 2023, I asked then general secretary of FEBA, Angela Frigo, about declining levels of surplus. Angela told me how FEBA were seeking alternative ways to source food to distribute to the 351 Food Banks in 30 European countries who make up their network: 'If we look at the planet it's good news because then it means that, well, we are reducing food waste. So that's the right direction. It's not good for the food banks because then it means that the quantities are decreasing, so we are getting less food.'

For FEBA, this decline has meant a pivot towards new ways of collecting surplus, including collecting leftover meals from restaurants, hotels, school canteens and even cruise ships:

> We started in 2018, then we had to stop due to the pandemic a project with Costa Cruceros, the cruise company. So you have to imagine these huge cruise ships preparing amazing food for the clients who are on holiday. We started in 2018 with Italy with a pilot test, then we replicated the system also in Marseille in France and in Barcelona in Spain. So the volunteers are recovering meals that are prepared but not served to clients. And so the following day when the ship is arriving in the harbour, the volunteers are collecting the food that was prepared the day before.

Angela explained that this way of collecting surplus isn't without its challenges, but has additional value as 'the quantities are lower, but at the same time that the quality is higher because you are recovering a meal. So, also in terms of nutritional value, it's higher, it's food which is ready that can be eaten immediately by the beneficiaries.'

I can understand the moral satisfaction – the moral imperative, even – of ensuring good quality food doesn't end up in the bin. But a monolith cruise ship docking in Barcelona or Marseille and offloading surplus food to people who are food insecure surely isn't the answer. A press release detailing the partnership claimed 'this initiative has managed to give a second life to more than 70,000 food servings'.[37]

Language is so important here – food is being given a 'second life', and the implied undertone suggests, 'Who can argue with that?' But is there really any dignity in giving out what are essentially cruise ship leftovers to hungry people? What are the logistics of ensuring the food arrives safely and in a presentable way? Are we talking actual meals or bits and pieces of random items leftover from the buffet? The very idea of food as a basic human right simply does not align with this form of redistribution. The waste generated on the ship is intended to give passengers an abundance of options. The 'second life' doesn't provide nearly as many choices due to the organisational dynamics mentioned earlier. One person's excess is another person's scarcity.

We have seen how the hunger industrial complex is thriving in North America, but can we slow down its advancement in the UK and other countries across Europe? The linkage of surplus and poverty as a 'win-win solution' appears to be an attractive one – an undeniable one, even. The growing digitalisation and technology linking surplus with charitable organisations offers one way of redirecting food, but at the same time the monetisation can lead to issues of competition between charities, scarcity and an inability to meet people's needs and ultimately fulfil their right to food. Critiquing the role of corporations in propping up and sustaining the 'emergency' charitable food aid system is a discussion that can cause discomfort and unease – especially for those on the front line, such as Marco at the Lazio Food Bank in Rome and Greg at WSCAH in New York City, who are navigating the donations that end up at their door. Yet it is necessary to uplift the problems inherent in the hunger industrial complex if we are to advocate for solutions that work towards societies where people have the right to access food with dignity and choice. Ending the need for charitable food aid involves reimagining the hierarchies of power that corporate-backed charity can reinforce, and that have often been strengthened by the pandemic, as Chapter 3 explores.

3

The Problems of Charitable Food Aid under a Permanent State of 'Emergency'

The Covid-19 pandemic showed us just how precarious the 'emergency' charitable food aid system really is, and its inadequacy in addressing chronic poverty and insecurity. Food started to run out rapidly. Volunteers, often retired and having to stay at home for health reasons during the peak of the pandemic, were thin on the ground. Food banks had to start buying food to fill the shelves in attempts to meet the ever-growing demand. In the Trussell network in the UK, purchased food has risen from 2 per cent of all distributed food in 2019–20 to 23 per cent in 2024–25.[1]

Originally, 'emergency' food aid via food banks and food pantries were established to respond to a short-term need. The onset of the pandemic in March 2020 drastically impacted the way the charitable food aid world operated, revealing the essential nature of this so-called emergency provision. There was a huge need that had to be met as quickly and safely as possible. Gone were the café-style food banks and pantries that offered a cup of tea and a chat. Socially distanced lines winding along pavements took their place. People had to grab and go. The 'emergency' framing necessitated in and out visits, less social contact and more social isolation. Visiting the US in October 2022, many organisations were still operating socially distanced food pantries and charitable food aid provision. Some needed medical details, masks to be worn and to know if I'd visited another state in the seven days before my visit. Organisations that had built up sociable and welcoming community spaces lost that aspect overnight. The knock-on effect of that was volunteers and workers no longer got to know people's situations and couldn't refer them on for support elsewhere.

As we grapple with a new reality defined by 'permacrisis', the expansion of 'emergency' food provision in the UK and other wealthy-yet-unequal nations has taken on a troubling permanence. The ongoing cost-of-living crisis, coupled with political instability and the deepening global food insecurity exacerbated by conflicts in Ukraine and Gaza – where food has been weaponised[2] – has solidified the entrenchment and corporatisation of food aid. It's a stark reminder that we must reframe our approach to charity, community and care.

'EMERGENCY' CHARITABLE FOOD AID

Emergency: something dangerous or serious, such as an accident, that happens suddenly or unexpectedly and needs fast action in order to avoid harmful results.

Considering this *Collins Dictionary* definition of an 'emergency' in relation to charitable food aid provision, it's obvious that what we are witnessing now is not an 'emergency' at all. Instead, it is chronic and embedded. As we pivot from one crisis to the next, 'emergency' charitable solutions are unable to address the deeply ingrained poverty and inequality that people are facing. Long-term solutions are needed that focus on providing people with an income that allows people to afford to buy, choose and eat the food they want, protecting their human right to food. 'Emergency' food provision is not addressing the root causes of poverty, and it is neither a dignified nor long-term solution.

Given the continued growth and reach of this type of provision, the idea of charitable food as an 'emergency' needs to be reframed. As *Sweet Charity* author Jan Poppendieck explained in relation to the growth of food charity in the US back in 1998, what started as a grassroots 'emergency' response soon developed into a seemingly permanent landscape of corporate-backed charity that absorbs food surpluses and relieves hunger *temporarily*. Now it is difficult to imagine a society without food banks, given their reach and visibility. This shift in the food charity landscape highlights the need for ongoing discussions about sustainability and long-term solutions.

Katie Martin is the CEO of More Than Food Consulting, LLC and author of *Reinventing Food Banks and Pantries*.[3] I travelled from New York City to Connecticut to meet Katie at Hands on Hartford, a social service non-profit organisation that serves Hartford's 'most economically challenged residents in the areas of food, housing, and health'.[4] Katie told me that her goal is to 'to create a paradigm shift in the charitable food system to move from short-term transactions of food to long-term transformations of lives'. She's worked with dozens of food banks and food pantries to help promote healthy food and address the root causes of food insecurity. One of the first things we discussed was the term 'emergency' being applied to charitable food provision. 'Let's stop using the term emergency when we talk about charitable food provision', Katie urged. 'It's time to shift our focus from an emergency response toward empowerment and from short-term transactions of food to long-term transformations of lives', Katie has written in *Reinventing Food Banks and Pantries*, in a shift from 'basic emergency services to advanced best practices'.[5]

A former staff member at Seattle's Food Lifeline, josh martinez (who intentionally spells his name with lowercase letters), agrees that we need to move away from the term 'emergency'. josh started his consultancy practice Future Emergent after leaving Food Lifeline in Seattle, a Feeding America food bank, where he was director of agency programmes and network development for over three years. One of the factors that led to josh setting up Future Emergent was that he saw first hand that 'food banks were not meeting the need'. At Food Lifeline, less than 5 per cent of his time on the job was spent recognising what needs to change.

When food banks began to emerge in the 1960s, 'emergency food' was the most appropriate name for the circumstances people were in at that time. Charitable food aid was a temporary solution to an acute, not a chronic, problem. Now, according to josh, 'organisations do not provide emergency food so much as they are providing *essential* food'. This perspective challenges us to rethink the role of food banks and charitable food aid, pushing beyond the idea of temporary relief. What does this imply for the way food banks and charitable food aid should function?

Reimagining spaces of charitable food aid is indicative of a central contradiction – do we make food banks better, or seek to end their existence for good? Or can we do both at once? There are inevitable power dynamics between volunteers and guests, shoppers, recipients, clients, neighbours or whatever term is being used to refer to people experiencing hunger. No matter how dignified workers and volunteers try to make the experience, ultimately it *is* undignified. There are rules, such as only taking two of a particular item. There are other kinds of regulations. Sometimes they're enforced, sometimes they're not. They evolve, constantly. There are expectations that you leave items on the shelves for the person 'shopping' after you. That doesn't happen in Sainsbury's or Walmart (apart from the restrictions we saw during Covid-19). How are people supposed to know from one week to the next what role they should play? Architects can design welcoming spaces, volunteers can be friendly and welcoming, and food can be high quality and fresh, but ultimately, charity is a gift, not an entitlement.

RESPONDING TO THE CRISIS

The pandemic exacerbated the rise of charitable food aid and led to dramatic increases in food insecurity in the Global North, especially for marginalised communities facing unique challenges tied to race, disability, gender and location.[6] As the crisis unfolded, existing inequalities became even more pronounced, leading to a huge spike in the number of people seeking emergency food aid. Millions suddenly found themselves without income or jobs, grappling with skyrocketing living costs. Food banks and charities, often thought of as safety nets for the most vulnerable, suddenly became overwhelmed with first-time users, exposing just how fragile our social support systems really are – even in affluent nations. The situation was made worse by supply chain disruptions, shortages of volunteers and rising food prices, all of which further strained resources. Marginalised communities – who were already at greater risk of experiencing poverty and food insecurity – felt the brunt of these challenges.

In response, governments and the private sector increased 'emergency' food aid initiatives but did not address the structural causes of food insecurity, further embedding charity as a false solution. In the UK, DEFRA pledged £16 million for FareShare and the Waste and Resources Action Programme, and a fund for smaller food distribution charities in England. This was the first time direct funding from the UK government was offered to food charity. In the US, the USDA announced an additional $850 million in Congressional coronavirus relief on top of standard funding for food banks.[7] The USDA also expanded the Meals-to-You public–private partnership, working with the Baylor Collaborative on Hunger and Poverty, McLane Global, PepsiCo and others to deliver more than one million meals a week to students in a limited number of rural schools closed due to Covid-19. Such corporate partnerships boomed, accompanied by gains in corporate social responsibility and perceived respectability – alongside hefty tax incentives to donate. *Big Hunger* author Andy Fisher found that all of the food banks in the Feeding America network gained considerable income during the pandemic. Feeding America's net worth in June 2019 increased by $440 million to $578 million in June 2022. As of 30 June 2022, it had $485 million in cash, up from $71 million in 2019; 192 food banks in Feeding America's network had about $7.4 billion in net assets as of their latest financial reports.[8]

In April 2020, the Canadian government announced up to CAD$100 million to Food Banks Canada and other food rescue organisations through the Emergency Food Security Fund to 'help improve access to food for people experiencing food insecurity due to the Covid-19 pandemic'.[9] These increased funds all sought to respond to the problem of increased food insecurity. But increased food insecurity is a symptom of deeper problems of inequality and inequity, and increasing the funds to food charities does not begin to address these underlying issues.

Increases in social security payments, such as the UK's £20 uplift to the benefit Universal Credit, led to a decrease in food insecurity overall. The Food Foundation compared food insecurity pre- and post-pandemic and reported food insecurity levels in households receiving Universal Credit were 37 per cent lower (43 per cent in 2019–21 compared with 27 per cent in 2020–1),[10] suggesting that the £20 made a real difference to families being able to afford the food they needed. But the impact of that wasn't felt evenly, with disabled people unable to access the temporary uplift at all.

Despite such temporary government interventions and increased public and corporate donations, the crisis exposed deep structural inequalities, laying bare both the critical importance of emergency food aid and the urgent need for long-term solutions to food insecurity. Academic Dan Warshawsky explains that the charitable food aid system 'was never designed for a crisis on this scale, yet it was often the first place people thought of when the crisis emerged'.[11]

In an increasingly precarious and demanding context, food aid providers were forced to adapt – quickly and creatively – to ensure people still had access to food. During my early field visits, pandemic restrictions were still in place at many pantries and food aid sites, limiting services such as sit-down meals that had been common before the crisis. In the US, organisations were still grappling with the fallout from the end of emergency pandemic supports, such as the SNAP Emergency Allotments, which had provided crucial extra funds to low-income families until March 2023.[12] Yet despite reduced resources, many groups continued to experiment with new models of food distribution: community fridges, drive-in digital pantries and swipe-card-access vending machines in SRO hotels stocked with fresh, culturally relevant meals. Drive-thru pantries, delivery services using apps such as DoorDash and Uber, and food lockers for contactless pickup quickly became part of the landscape.

When I first visited North America in October 2022 and again in May 2023, the legacy of the pandemic was still shaping daily operations. On 11 May 2023, as we drove to the Open Bible pantry in Portland, Oregon, the radio announced that today was the official end of the pandemic in the US. That morning, we met Executive Director Betty Brown and her son Aaron, the church's minister, who described how they had restructured their pantry during the crisis – shifting to an online ordering system and a drive-thru pickup in the church parking lot. Portland Open Bible food pantry was created in 2015 to address the lack of food access in southeast Portland. Betty, a registered nurse and huge believer in 'food as medicine', explained how their neighbourhood is incredibly diverse, with large Russian, Chinese, Vietnamese and Latinx communities. The idea for the food pantry came about after the church was broken into three times in a short period. Each time, the only thing that was stolen was food, not any of the expensive computer equipment. Betty realised that there was an unmet need in their community. 'We're one of the most underserved areas in the state', she pointed out.

In just ten years, the pantry grew from serving 123 families in 2013 to 84,000 families in 2023. Betty emphasised, 'We've never made food boxes'. It's essential for people to choose what they want, especially given the diverse needs in the community. With the onset of the pandemic, they were determined not to take away that choice by resorting to pre-made boxes. This led to the creation of the drive-thru digital pantry. In October 2020, they developed an online system that allowed people to pre-order the food they needed, which volunteers then assembled into boxes. People were given specific time slots to drive into the parking lot and collect their food. Betty and Aaron proudly recalled the time they had 150 cars come through in two hours!

The online ordering system could be translated into Russian, Cantonese, Spanish, Arabic, Vietnamese and English. I asked how they made sure people received culturally relevant food, and Betty told me: 'We always have people from the particular culture packing the boxes, so people who are Spanish know which beans people will want.' The nearby Providence Medical Centre partnered with the church to put a pantry in their clinic. Every two weeks, Betty received a report on the diversity of ethnicities they're serving and what they're choosing to eat so they can tailor their offering. The people accessing the drive-thru pantry are mostly people who are working but living in poverty, Betty said. They're often embarrassed, and also don't have the time to spend waiting in line. For disabled people, the drive-thru pantry offers a more convenient option that's 'opened the door to more people being able to access food'.

After we finished chatting with Betty and Aaron, they offered to show us how the pantry worked. A car was being loaded up by a young volunteer as we headed across the parking lot. Aaron, who coordinates the pantry, explained how each item is numbered and sorted into bags. Then the volunteer just takes the numbered bag from the freezer, fridge or table. We walked into a room filled with brown paper bags bursting with amazing looking produce. I had a look at one of the labels – it had the person's name, number, time slot and list of the food they'd chosen. Potatoes, apples, oranges, tomatoes, peppers, watermelon, courgettes – the quality of the food was incredible. They also add printed leaflets about accessing public or inexpensive healthcare in the bags, as it's a good way to reach people who may not be aware of their options. The fridges were fully stocked with milk, dairy and non-dairy, and lots of eggs. I hadn't seen so many eggs for ages as we'd had a shortage in the UK for months.

Looking at the rows of fresh produce and neatly packed bags, I couldn't help thinking: this level of care and dignity shouldn't be exceptional, it should be the norm. Access to good quality, culturally relevant food still depends far too much on where you live, the colour of your skin, your mobility and your income. This is what activists and organisers mean when they talk about food apartheid – not a 'food desert' but a system of racialised and class-based segregation in access to nourishment.

FOOD APARTHEID

The role of corporations in deepening the structural inequalities that limit access to healthy food became even more apparent to me during a visit to Syracuse, New York, in June 2024. Syracuse has the highest child poverty rate of any mid-sized city in the US, and its Black residents face the sixth-highest poverty rate among US cities with populations over 100,000.[13] I was there for a week, attending the US National Community of Practice Right to Food annual summit. The summit focused on the lived experiences of residents from Syracuse's predominantly Black and Brown South and West Sides, bringing together community organisers and activists from across the US to highlight the systems and institutions that keep food insecurity alive in high-poverty neighbourhoods.

Throughout the summit, the term 'food apartheid' was regularly used to describe these systemic inequalities. The term was coined by Karen Washington, a Bronx-based activist and urban farmer, to describe the structural, race-based inequalities in America's food system. A 'food desert', the terminology often used to describe an area with limited access to plentiful, affordable or nutritious food, suggests a natural phenomenon – something that has occurred by chance. 'Food apartheid', by contrast, fully gets at the intentionality and structural racism that leads to people living in Black, Indigenous and People of Colour (BIPOC) communities struggling to access fresh, readily available and culturally relevant produce. Speaking in *The Guardian* in 2021, Karen Washington explained:

> There's a stigma attached to terms like food desert which disenfranchises and disempowers so many of us. It's only helpful for bureaucrats and statisticians, it doesn't get to the root problem which is hunger and poverty. The fact is the food system is racist, and access to food is based on color of skin, how much money you have and where you live. Deserts are natural and have food, food deserts are manmade, not natural. Food is a human right. It's not natural for people to be living this way and eating this way.[14]

Food apartheid acknowledges the racial, economic and structural barriers that limit access to healthy food, particularly for BIPOC communities. What that looked like in Syracuse was big corporate retailers closing and leaving gaping holes in food access for residents. Major chain supermarkets are often reluctant to locate their stores in low-income BIPOC neighbourhoods, a practice known as supermarket redlining,[15] evoking policies designed to prevent Black home ownership in white neighbourhoods and promote segregation.

Food access is also deeply tied to socio-economic status. Visiting rural West Virginia in October 2023, the difficulties in accessing healthy, nutritious food were strikingly apparent. West Virginia has the greatest rate of food insecurity in the country, affecting over 15 per cent of the population. Approximately 50 per cent of West Virginians live in rural areas, compared to the national average of about 20 per cent.[16] Rural residents live further from public services than those in urban areas and have less access to public transportation, greatly impacting their ability to access good food. I don't want to use the term 'food desert', but how can we describe what is happening in rural states such as West Virginia? The terminology 'food swamp', defined as 'environments saturated with unhealthy foods because of the large numbers of corner stores and fast-food outlets in them',[17] has been used to refer to the proliferation of unhealthy food options in communities. But this terminology reinforces place-based stigma and attaches negative connotations to areas already impacted by stereotypical tropes and deep-seated poverty.

Essentially, the rise of stores such as Family Dollar and Dollarama – now some of the fastest-growing food retailers in North America – in states such as West Virginia are endangering communities' right to adequate and nutritious food. Food might be affordable, but it lacks nutrition and does little to address high food insecurity rates. These stores are disproportionately located in low-income, rural and Black areas,[18] perpetuating systemic racial and socio-economic inequalities.

Choice and access to healthy, nutritious food was also what inspired Maria Aldarete to form Community Kitchens Oakland in California as part of a mission to build community and solidarity through food by 'meeting communities where they are'. Maria told me about her 'tremendous connection to Oakland', having been part of the community for 30 years. She was working minimum wage jobs and living from one payday to the next before she built a successful business, Luka's Taproom & Lounge, which was forced to permanently close in 2022 as a result of a rent dispute. Maria started Community Kitchens one week after the lockdowns began in March 2020. Community Kitchens quickly became known for its free and accessible meal programme. She worked on her own in the organisation for two years without giving herself any sort of salary.

Speaking to Maria in May 2023, there were four staff members, but – as is the case for so many of the organisations I've visited – they need more funding to meet the growing need they're seeing. Their Community Kitchen Home Chef Program sees fresh, nutritious, home-cooked meals from restaurants and volunteer home chefs being delivered to six Town Fridges, which are found in some of the most food insecure neighbourhoods in Oakland, such as Deep East Oakland where I met Maria. The Town Fridges are extremely popular. Maria told me there are often lines stretching two to three blocks, and the food is almost inevitably gone within 20 minutes.

There was a huge growth in these sorts of mutual aid activities during the pandemic.[19] Mutual aid networks played a critical role in addressing food insecurity by organising community-based food distributions and meal deliveries. These grassroots efforts often filled gaps left by overwhelmed government programmes, emphasising solidarity over charity. Local farms, restaurants and volunteers collaborated to ensure people on the lowest incomes had consistent access to nutritious food. In the US, mutual aid has a long tradition in Black, immigrant and anarchist communities. Key to these historically significant mutual aid societies is that they are place-based and founded on neighbours helping neighbours within the same community.

Perhaps the most well-known example of mutual aid is the Black Panther party's breakfast programmes, which fed 20,000 children in cities across the US in 1969. Founded in Oakland, California, the Free Breakfast Program exemplified solidarity and community joy by providing children with nutritious meals, fostering a sense of empowerment and care within underserved neighbourhoods. Rather than charity, the programme was an act of mutual upliftment, demonstrating the power of collective action to meet basic needs while affirming dignity and self-determination. Their movement inspired people to build a shared analysis of poverty and structural racism by linking systemic oppression to capitalist exploitation, framing these issues as interconnected forces that perpetuated inequality.[20] Through community programmes and political education, the Black Panthers highlighted the ways institutional racism and economic deprivation denied Black communities access to basic rights such as food, housing, education and healthcare.[21] By engaging directly with affected communities, they fostered collective understanding and mobilised grassroots efforts to challenge these structures.

Based on the premise of solidarity, not charity, the pandemic led to a surge in grassroots groups offering peer-to-peer shopping and cooking support, setting up community fridges like the one I tried to visit in Oakland, and working tirelessly to pick up the pieces of the ongoing pandemic fallout. A common theme among all of the initiatives mentioned above was the commitment to offering people choice and nutritious food in communities where they are struggling to access it.

RESPONDING TO POVERTY, HUNGER AND TRAUMA

In the US, the lack of universal free healthcare was cited as an insurmountable barrier to people being able to escape poverty. 'Healthcare is causing poverty', Maria told me frankly. 'The majority of bankruptcies occur due to medical expenses', she continued. In fact, nearly 66 per cent of bankruptcies are linked to healthcare costs,[22] highlighting how a sudden medical emergency can plunge families into financial turmoil. The high cost of healthcare, coupled with inadequate insurance coverage, means that even middle-class families can find themselves in dire situations after a health crisis. Many people are forced to make difficult choices between paying for essential medical treatments and meeting their basic living expenses, such as housing and food, exacerbating health inequalities among marginalised communities already facing barriers to accessing care.

Across the towns and cities I visited in North America and Europe, it was clear just how much ill health and poverty are deeply connected to food insecurity. The resultant trauma that many people in the charitable and community food aid space are experiencing is widespread. Several of the organisations I visited were being led by trauma-informed approaches, which acknowledge how exposure to violence and trauma have broad and long-lasting effects on emotional, physical and financial health. These effects are often experienced unevenly, disproportionately affecting women, individuals from BIPOC backgrounds, disabled people and those from working-class backgrounds.

The overlapping of extreme poverty and ill health – both mental and physical – creates a perfect storm for people trying to live on the lowest incomes. In the UK, Carl Walker and colleagues have written about 'hunger trauma' as a unique experience in that 'it leads to feelings of emotional distress and guilt while also affecting people's sense of identity and status'.[23] Mariana Chilton explores a similar concept in *The Painful Truth about Hunger in America*,[24] where she discusses intergenerational trauma. She explains how the effects of hunger extend far beyond immediate physical discomfort, often accumulating over generations. This trauma can manifest in a variety of ways, impacting mental health, community cohesion and social stability. Chilton highlights that 'the experience of hunger is rooted in trauma and gender-based violence', underscoring how systemic issues, such as poverty and inequality, intersect with personal experiences of violence and trauma. Chilton notes that the legacy of hunger is often intertwined with a history of abuse, neglect or systemic oppression, leading to a cycle that is difficult to break. Women and children often bear the brunt of these compounded traumas. Acknowledging the profound psychological and emotional dimensions of hunger, Chilton advocates for a holistic approach to food security – one that incorporates trauma-informed care, community support and policies aimed at dismantling the structural barriers that keep individuals and families trapped in such cycles of deprivation and distress.

Nourishing Hope in Chicago is one of the organisations adopting a trauma-informed approach to food insecurity. Their approach acknowledges the complex emotional and psychological impacts of trauma on people's lives, particularly people who are accessing charitable food aid. Nourishing Hope's Sheridan Market food pantry is located in an affluent neighbourhood close to the waterfront in Chicago. Senior Manager of Pantry Programs Angela Cimarusti-Clifford and Chief Program Officer Jennie Hull showed me around the pantry, which was a $3.5 million redevelopment designed by architects (who have since become known for designing food pantries). The pantry looks so much like a regular shop 'we once had a businessman in a suit who got off the L[25] from work and came to us as he thought we were a store!', Jenny said. Walking in, there are bunches of flowers displayed on the wall, ready for clients to take home with them when they arrive for their prepicked parcel of food they've already ordered online.

Upstairs, there are several rooms used for free counselling and therapy sessions. The rooms are delicately lit, with bowls of brightly coloured fidget toys ready for people to use. There's also a social services office. 'How do people do this without support?' Jenny asked. During the pandemic, the city of Chicago closed all mental health services. Nourishing Hope have five full-time therapists on staff, as well as mental health interns. There's still a six-to-eight-month wait for counselling. It's completely free and all opt-in, and the staff don't decide who gets counselling. Workers and volunteers receive training on non-violent crisis intervention. 'It's important to be consistent, to offer choice, and to build that trust', Jenny said, adding, 'All of us had some form of trauma during the pandemic'.

Something I heard regularly during my visit to Chicago in May 2024 was how people seeking refuge and asylum were coming from Texas and arriving in the city, having been 'put on a bus and promised the world', as Jenny put it. The thousands of people arriving in the city were at times having to live in police stations, churches and hotels downtown as there was nowhere else for them to go. Often, people weren't allowed to bring food into these spaces, increasing their already high risk of hunger and food insecurity. For almost 40 years, Chicago has been a self-proclaimed 'sanctuary city'.[26] Although the term does not have a precise legal definition, it is a broad term used for any city or county (or state) that has policies or practices in place aimed at limiting involvement in federal immigration enforcement actions.[27] In August 2022, the Republican Texas governor Greg Abbott started to send people seeking refuge and asylum to Chicago. Since then, Chicago has welcomed over 44,000 new arrivals from the southern border. On almost every street corner, I would see women with young children sitting outside stores, selling sweets and tissues, trying to make a few dollars. I was told that the women were mostly Venezuelan asylum seekers who had arrived in the city and were trying to get by.

Jenny told me that the increase in newcomers to the pantry was causing friction at Sheridan Market. People accessing the pantry started to become aggressive for the first time. Tensions were evident as people queued up outside. Arguments started, and someone had pulled a knife on a member of staff, so they had to employ a security guard – something they were reluctant to do as it wasn't the sort of atmosphere they were keen to foster. 'We're dealing with crisis after crisis', Jenny continued. The fraught desperation of the scarcity mindset was causing othering and judgements about deservingness, and creating a situation where stigma flourishes. Volunteers and workers were trying their best to respond to the food, health and housing insecurity that people faced, but the precarity that characterises the emergency charitable food system resulted in a scarcity mindset that perpetuates these insecurities.

RESPONDING TO THE PUBLIC HEALTH EMERGENCY

Poor diet is one of the biggest preventable risk factors for ill health, with inequalities in diets contributing to inequalities in health overall.[28] Amid the crises in the charitable food aid system, there is a growing focus on providing healthier options and respecting individual choice. Many of the food pantries, food banks and community organisations I visited were focusing on offering the best quality, healthiest food possible, often with over 60 per cent fruit and vegetables in a food parcel or food box. This is especially important when we think of the 'food apartheid' and segregation that communities, especially BIPOC and working-class communities, can face when trying to access healthy food in their neighbourhoods.

The link between good quality nutrition and health has taken off massively in the form of 'food is medicine' in the US, which has spread to Canada and the UK in the form of prescription fruit and vegetable programmes. Food is medicine programmes, including produce prescriptions and medically tailored meals, use food-based interventions to help prevent, manage and treat diet-related diseases. In 2024, the Rockefeller Foundation committed $80 million to further advance Food is Medicine in the US.[29]

The Food Bank of Central and Eastern North Carolina has been working with state healthcare providers to deliver food and/or produce prescriptions to 500 patients. Chris Costanzo, founder and editor of *Food Bank News*, explains how the food bank expect to be earning $2 million a month by serving 14,000 patients through North Carolina's Medicaid 1115 waiver,[30] which allows health insurers to reimburse organisations when they provide non-medical interventions, such as food or housing, to improve patient health. Gideon Adams, vice president of community health and engagement at the Food Bank of Central and Eastern North Carolina, referred to some of the 'labor-intensive' issues around the billing and administration of the programme, but stressed the opportunities in being able to rely on government insurance funding to address food insecurity. 'We're talking about a potential funding stream that's the size of the defense budget', he said. 'It's huge, with a huge need.'[31]

The first UK trial of GPs prescribing fruit and vegetables has shown promising results, leading to the charity behind the project to call for nationwide programmes to boost health and reduce food poverty. The Alexandra Rose Charity has trialled fruit and vegetables on prescription pilots in two London Boroughs, with initial results suggesting a 'profound impact … on the lives of people on low incomes, living with long-term health conditions linked to poor diet'.[32] According to the evaluation of the trial, after just eight months of receiving vouchers for fruit and vegetables, 80 per cent of participants were eating five portions of fruit and vegetables each day, compared to just 28 per cent at the start of the programme. Over half of participants shared that their mental health had also improved as they worried less about money for food. In Canada, food insecurity researchers Val Tarasuk and Lynn McIntyre have noted their concerns about the longevity of these types of prescription schemes: 'The temporary effect of food pre-scription programmes on participants' household food insecurity begs the question of what if any of the documented benefits from these programmes can be sustained beyond the duration of the prescriptions?'[33]

Are prescription programmes just another temporary stop gap measure, like food banks and food pantries? While such pro-grammes can potentially provide short-term relief, they fail to address the root causes of food insecurity, such as poverty and systemic inequalities. They can also exclude groups without access to healthcare, which could lead to inequalities in access geograph-ically. Such programmes also risk framing hunger as an individual problem rather than a consequence of broader economic and policy issues. A more effective approach would focus on prevent-ing food insecurity at its root, rather than relying on yet further temporary measures.

I observed first hand how the goal of offering fresh produce could come into conflict with the unstable housing situations of those seeking help. While volunteering at the Nourish East End food bank in Toronto, I worked in the fruit and vegetable section of the church basement, which operated like a market-style food bank. During this time, I met several men living alone who didn't want to take any vegetables. If people were living in shared accommodation or SROs, which are typically developed from older hotel buildings and aimed at people living on a low income, seniors and people experiencing homelessness, then cooking facilities aren't always readily available.

In San Francisco, I visited Farming Hope to join one of their regular community dinners. I met Ram Olivares-Ochoa, associate director of Community Food Programs, who told me about a pilot programme with the Conard House SRO, who offer housing for people who have experienced homelessness and/or chronic mental health conditions. The pilot programme involved a vending machine stocked with fresh, healthy microwavable meals that residents could access via a swipe card, three meals a day, four days a week. When I returned home from my trip, Ram sent me a photograph of the vending machine so I could see how it looked. 'Good food, good mood' is written across the top of the spotlessly clean fridge, which is packed with fresh meals that residents can take away and heat up.

This focus on accessible, nutritious food reminded me of other organisations I visited, which were also prioritising healthy, seasonal, locally grown and culturally relevant produce for communities, often at a nominal fee. Community Supported Agriculture (CSA) is a subscription for a box of fresh, seasonal, locally grown vegetables that can be picked up directly from a farm. CSA supports small-scale farmers through long-term partnerships: a farmer offers a certain number of 'shares' to the public, which typically consist of a box of vegetables; a community of members covers the cost of production and receives a share of the harvest throughout the season in return.

The role of CSA in addressing food insecurity and injustice in the food system was something I grew increasingly interested in as I visited urban farms. One such farm is Zenger Farm, located in Powellhurst-Gilbert – one of the most ethnically, racially and culturally diverse neighbourhoods in Oregon – where I went to learn more about their unique CSA Partnerships for Health, led by Eric Rodriguez. The programme, which delivers CSA shares to low-income families affected by diet-related illness in an effort to address issues of food access and health disparities in Multnomah County, is unique to Zenger Farm. Partnerships for Health offers a creative, engaging solution to improve food access and focuses on preventing ill health by turning community health centres into vibrant neighbourhood spaces that distribute food from local farms. Patients receive fresh, locally grown vegetables each week in their CSA box, which are available for pick up at a local clinic or delivered to their doorstep via DoorDash, a company that provides online food ordering and food delivery, similar to Uber Eats.

Each box includes enough produce for up to four people, healthy recipes and information on new ways to prepare their produce, and costs $5 a week paid in cash or SNAP, for food worth around $25. It's essential that the share offers culturally relevant food that the diverse client base love to eat, such as little green tomatillos, which originated in Central America and have been a staple in Latin American cuisine for centuries. Speaking to Eric in May 2023, he told me that farmers receive $700 a share for 22 weeks, twice a year. The farmers are from local family farms who prioritise inclusive labour policies and farming with natural practices. This model not only supports local agriculture but fosters a more sustainable, equitable food system for the community.

Before Covid-19, clinic pickups would be staffed by farmers, community health workers and programme interns who were there to answer any questions about the produce. Adapting to the trials of the pandemic using rideshare services such as DoorDash wasn't without its challenges. Not only was the social element of the programme lost but there were also physical barriers to clients receiving their share. Sometimes they said the food didn't turn up. Zenger staff had to drive to each client's house to map out the area for delivery drivers. Is there a locked gate? Does the buzzer work? 'Every week there is some glitch', Eric said. 'It's a juggling act. We always feel like we're behind.'

Most CSA members tend to be demographically homogenous, with members being women, white, highly educated and affluent. In contrast, Zenger's CSA Partnerships for Health successfully – and intentionally – reached a racially and socio-economically diverse population.[34] A bilingual veggie guide in Spanish and English is included in the box, with suggestions for how to use the produce. Eric said this is especially important in the winter share as there are items such as greens, chicory, endive and different squashes that people often haven't cooked with before.

While programmes such as CSA Partnerships for Health can enhance both physical and mental well-being for participants, challenges persist. Funding and scaling these small-scale models remain significant hurdles. These initiatives often struggle to secure consistent, sustainable financial backing, limiting their ability to reach larger populations or offer long-term solutions. Broader systemic issues also come into play. As mentioned earlier, many organisations depend on surplus donations from supermarkets and corporations, leading to inconsistent food variety and quality. There are additional concerns around the ethical implications of depending on corporate donations, as it perpetuates the role of big businesses in shaping food systems that prioritise profit over people's health and well-being.

When reimagining food assistance beyond charity, it's important to retain key elements that foster community and dignity. The social connections built into food spaces are essential for combating isolation and creating networks that go beyond just food provision. The care, respect and humanity shown by front-line workers and volunteers affirm people's inherent dignity, countering the stigma often associated with food insecurity. Access to high-quality, nutritious and culturally relevant food is crucial, respecting diverse dietary needs and traditions. Sharing cooking knowledge and food preparation skills in non-hierarchical, non-judgemental spaces empowers people beyond simply receiving meals. The most transformative approach would preserve these vital elements of food charity, shifting away from the giver–receiver dynamic towards a model of collective care and resource sharing, while simultaneously working towards systemic changes that eventually render food charity unnecessary.

4

Labour Exploitation and Burnout in the Charitable Food Aid System

Because of you, someone will eat today.

Walking into the cavernous 'orientation room' for my volunteering shift at the Greater Chicago Food Depository, the quotation above was one of many peppered across the bright white walls. Motivational quotes from Martin Luther King and Mahatma Gandhi stretched around every corner of the room. Tiered lecture hall-style seats ran along the length of the back wall, and in front were rows of neat green cubes for volunteers to sit on as they're guided through what happens once the shift starts.

I'd signed up for a repack shift at the Greater Chicago Food Depository (GCFD), which partners with over 800 partner organisations and programmes, including food pantries, soup kitchens, shelters and mobile distribution programmes in the Cook County region. I'd tried to meet with some of the staff at GCFD but received an email reply stating, 'As with most nonprofits, my colleagues and I often regretfully find ourselves stretched thin'. I decided to sign up for a volunteering shift instead. I arrived early and checked in on an iPad in the shiny entrance hall, which had opened in April 2024 a few weeks before my visit. On the walls, there were custom-made portraits of the food bank founders, alongside ceiling art inspired by staff quotes on hunger. I was welcomed by a smiling volunteer coordinator in a GCFD T-shirt who showed me to the orientation room. He told me they have around 70 volunteers every shift, twice a day. Many of the volunteers come from corporations and often from local schools. The day I volunteered, there were two different groups of excited school kids in the orientation room.

Once we're all in the hall, the 'orientation' begins. We're asked to give ourselves a round of applause – the first of many I encountered during the shift – before a show of hands to signal who has volunteered before. About half of the group, including all the school kids, had volunteered previously. A Powerpoint presentation in both English and Spanish encouraged us to take videos or photos of ourselves at work and tag GCFD in our photos, using the hashtags #Hungrytohopeful and #Endhungernow. We're told if we volunteer ten times we get a free T-shirt. Looking around, some people are clearly seasoned volunteers. Normally, I cheekily ask if I can have a T-shirt when I'm volunteering, but I don't want to disrupt the rules here as a one-time only volunteer. We're told music will be playing while we're working, and to share any song requests with one of the volunteer coordinators. The whole set up is incredibly polished.

There was a choice to repack bread or potatoes, and I chose the latter. Our group were led down a hall towards a huge sink where we had to wash our hands and put on plastic gloves, an apron and a hairnet before getting to work. There were four of us per table and we needed to pack potatoes into red plastic net bags ready to be distributed to one of the over 800 organisations the food bank serves. If any of the donated potatoes from local farms were past their best and needed composting, we had a box to throw them in.

I was packing next to Jenni,[1] who worked in real estate in downtown Chicago and started volunteering after her company did a Christmas holidays food donation drive. Her company allows her two days per month to volunteer, so she comes here as she finds she 'gets a lot out of helping others'. Jenni had a branded T-shirt. She offered to take some photos of me volunteering when I told her why I was there. The music was blasting. The school kids were darting around filling plastic boxes with potatoes and delivering them to our tables, eager to help us pack the potatoes for distribution. Amid the buzz, a volunteer coordinator stood nearby with a microphone, encouraging everyone to celebrate their efforts. 'Big up yourselves!', she called out, urging us to give ourselves a round of applause for lending a hand to 'our neighbours' in need. Packing donated potatoes to Gwen Stefani's 'Rich Girl' had a certain irony that wasn't lost on me.

The shift was non-stop. My hands were blistered due to sweat from wearing plastic gloves and the heavy lifting involved. Most of the potatoes were in good condition, and we were encouraged to try and win the 'biggest potato of the day competition'. The two volunteers across the table from me were mostly quiet throughout the shift, but when they saw the huge potato I'd put to one side to see if our table could win, they became animated. We did, in fact, come second in the competition.

The whole experience was so well put together, so organised, so corporate. It's hard to imagine a time when this wouldn't be here. I received an email the next day reiterating what we'd been told in the end-of-shift group huddle the day before:

Hello Repack Team,

Here are the totals for your May 29th, morning Repack session:

• 12,800 lbs. of Potatoes, which is 10,667 meals, which means you each did 144 meals per volunteer.

• 3,588 lbs. of Labeled Goods, which is 2,990 meals, which means you each did 299 meals per volunteer.

• 1,440 lbs. of Bread, which is 1,200 meals, which means you each did 120 meals per volunteer.

For a grand total of 17,857 lbs. of Food Repacked!

And a grand total of 14,857 Meals Repacked!

Great Job Team!

Thank you all for your support!

Your support helps us provide food and peace of mind for individuals and families throughout Cook County. Today, you helped us make an immediate impact in your community.

Thank you again for serving today. Together we can take hunger off the table. Together we are Greater!

FURTHER YOUR IMPACT

Advocate

The Covid-19 pandemic has deepened hunger and inequality. Help us strengthen the essential food assistance programmes that are protecting individuals from hunger and ensure all Illinoisans have food on the table. Send a message to your Members of Congress.

I struggled to make the connection between the potatoes I'd been bagging and the '144 meals' figure that was being suggested. I was interested to see the encouragement to advocate in the email, which was missing from the volunteering experience itself.

Even just from one shift, it was obvious that there is a huge amount of labour – physical, emotional and moral – involved in providing and maintaining charitable food aid systems. Such labour is often unpaid, and even when it is paid, it can be precarious and insecure.

KEEPING THE CHARITABLE FOOD AID SYSTEM GOING

I've often wondered how powerful it would be if it was possible to put a monetary figure on the extent of the work being done by volunteers in charitable food aid spaces. Back in 2017, Trussell and IFAN calculated that volunteers across the UK were giving 'at least £30 million' a year in unpaid work to support food banks.[2] In the US, 68 per cent of food pantries and 42 per cent of soup kitchens in Feeding America's national network are entirely reliant on volunteers. Approximately two million Feeding America network volunteers provided more than 8.4 million hours of service each month in 2012. If these volunteers were paid at the prevailing federal minimum wage of $7.25 per hour, their work would cost more than $60 million in monthly wages.[3] At the European FEBA, there are '97,940 co-workers of whom 93 percent were volunteers', according to their website.[4]

Keeping charitable food aid spaces going requires enormous levels of care and commitment from both paid and unpaid workers. Trussell CEO Emma Revie told me that the majority of their food bank volunteers across the UK are aged between 55 and 80, with 65 per cent identifying as women and 35 per cent as men. Moreover, 55 per cent of volunteers identify as Christian. About one-third of the volunteers had been volunteering for over five years, while the average time that they give per week is 15 hours. In her ethnographic research in a food pantry in New York City, Maggie Dickinson, author of *Feeding the Crisis: Care and Abandonment in America's Food Safety Net*, observes that 'like all caring labor, volunteer work in soup kitchens and food pantries is shaped by race, class, and gender inequalities'.[5]

Volunteering in charitable food aid settings constitutes a space of structural advantage, as white, middle-class individuals are often the people with the time and resources to engage in unpaid labour. This is in stark contrast to the people receiving charitable food provision, particularly women, racialised groups and people seeking refuge and asylum, who experience a disproportionate burden of hunger due to ongoing legacies of racial, colonial and patriarchal violence.[6] Rebecca de Souza, author of *Feeding the Other: Whiteness, Privilege, and Neoliberal Stigma in Food Pantries*, argues that:

> A key problem with charity is that it results in outpourings of gratitude on the part of givers, but never quite moves in the direction of food justice. Charity allows white middle-class women to reach out to the Other and to feel sadness for the Other, while also summoning up intense emotions linked to personal gratitude – as heard in the oft-repeated refrain: 'I am just so grateful for what I have'.[7]

The CEO of Future Emergent in Seattle, josh martinez, created a series of recommendations for the Washington State Department of Agriculture to improve their Emergency Food Assistance Program,[8] which funds hundreds of food banks and pantries across Washington State. A central part of his recommendations focus on repositioning values towards food justice and the right to food. According to josh, people in the food-banking industry view food assistance in two broad camps:

> One group of people generally sees the food-banking system as emergency food: supplemental, temporary, and incomplete. We give what we can, but we don't have the resources to provide long-term assistance. Another group generally sees the food-banking system as providing essential food: complete, nutritious, and ongoing. They may see hunger as a symptom of poverty, which itself is driven by racism, classism, or both. Ending hunger means ending the root causes of hunger. There's a spectrum of nuance between these two groups; people may have their own

perspective that adopts beliefs from one or more camps. Many of the issues we face as an industry stem from tension between people along this spectrum.

Often, the organisations I visited had workers who were either previously or currently experiencing food insecurity themselves. Dickinson explains how volunteer work can be both personally and politically motivated. It is often the result of 'deep poverty and need', resulting in volunteering in charitable food aid spaces becoming 'an economic lifeline ... volunteers in the context of weakened welfare protections, widespread economic insecurity, and growing precarity in the United States'.[9]

Workers and volunteers often knew what it was like to experience precarity in terms of low pay, housing insecurity and hunger. The horizontality and sense of solidarity that came from their collective experience was an integral part of the dignity they were seeking to offer. But the ever-increasing need – which shows no signs of letting up – meant that volunteers are often propping up a system that is barely relieving food insecurity, even temporarily. Charlotte White, former food bank manager and Member Support Officer for IFAN, has reflected on the 'food bank paradox':

When I was managing the food bank [Earlsfield, in south-west London], it often felt like running on a treadmill that was getting faster and faster. There was no time to stop or even pause and catch a breath. After a busy session, it was straight into planning the next one. And with this exhaustion often came a bit of guilt. This just felt wrong. The harder we worked and the busier we got, the more it felt like we were enabling the normalisation of food banks as a solution to poverty. I felt this each time we put out messages on social media, asking for donations or new volunteers. Was it just reinforcing the message that food banks are here to stay?[10]

The ubiquitous presence of precarious funding arrangements must have been mentioned to me at virtually every organisation I visited. It wasn't just the smaller, grassroots organisations that were struggling with funding cuts. Many larger organisations who received an influx of funding during the pandemic found themselves struggling once that funding was withdrawn. 'Covid created new empires of charitable food aid', Kathryn Scharf at Community Food Centres Canada in Toronto told me. Angela Cimarusti-Clifford at Nourishing Hope in Chicago agreed, stating that 'money was falling from the sky for us' during the pandemic.

This led to new and innovative ways of providing food being offered, such as the pop-up pantry run by the San Francisco-Marin Food Bank, where I volunteered one morning. I arrived early, and there was already a long snaking queue of people waiting along one side of the pavement. Previously, volunteers used to pre-bag the food, but now stations are set up and people can choose, farmers market style. What this meant in practice, however, was volunteers placing the items in people's shopping trolleys – people weren't allowed to pick it up themselves.

In just two hours, we'd served 593 families. It was demanding, physical work. Back at my hotel that night, I calculated that I'd lifted 537 kg of rice. Visiting the San Francisco-Marin Food Bank warehouse after my shift, I was told that there were waitlists at every single one of the more than 20 pop-up pantries across the city. Despite the constant demand, in October 2023 it was announced that due to budget cuts, the San Francisco-Marin Food Bank would be scaling down their pandemic-era services over the next two years, resulting in the closure of all emergency pop-up pantries by the end of June 2025. This also involves the loss of staff jobs, with the food bank anticipating its staffing level would fall from 253 to fewer than 200 employees. The precarity of the charitable food aid system thus affects not just those seeking food but also those on the front line keeping the broken system going.

BURNOUT AND PRECARITY

Volunteers and those working on the front lines risk becoming burned out as a result of the complex physical, emotional and moral labour involved in maintaining the charitable food aid system. UK food banks have brought in counsellors and private GPs to help exhausted workers and volunteers cope with the stress and exhaustion triggered by the explosion in demand for emergency food.[11] More than 2,000 Trussell food bank staff and volunteers can access a package of health and well-being support, including help with compassion fatigue, mental health first aid, face-to-face appointments with GPs and counsellors, and access to a helpline provided by the Samaritans. In October 2022, 3,000 people who run, volunteer and work in emergency food providers in communities across the UK signed a letter to the prime minister calling for urgent action to end the need for charitable food aid by ensuring everyone has enough income from work and social security. The letter stressed: 'Many of our teams are struggling to cope as demand for our support outstrips our food and financial donations and we are forced to make difficult decisions about how we operate. We are overstretched and exhausted. Many of our organisations are at breaking point.'[12]

In September 2023, Sabine Goodwin, Director of IFAN, told me:

Food banks have been finding that they can't necessarily support everyone, and they've had to find ways of rationing support. Even if they haven't yet, they're having to contemplate that because they don't see how they can keep going at the rate that they have been if demand was to increase. And more recently, what's happened is volunteer exhaustion and burnout for volunteers and food bank staff who are not only having to physically move food around, but they're dealing with more and more complex cases that they don't have the resources, in terms of knowledge and emotional capacity and can't necessarily then get the training or the information to help with the increasingly complex cases that are coming their way.

In the US, those working on the front lines are also facing precarity in terms of low-paid, insecure employment in food banks. This led to the San Francisco-Marin Food Bank becoming the first food bank in the US to unionise. Following my shift at the pop-up pantry, I headed straight to the San Francisco-Marin Food Bank to meet Emily Citraro, the department operations coordinator, to find out about what had led to their unionisation. Emily explained how she started working for the food bank back in 2001. Since then, she's worked in lots of roles. She told me how the union started pre-pandemic in response to poor working conditions in the organisation and made progress when Covid-19 set in.

Staff were working long hours, responding to the increased demands of food insecure people during the pandemic, risking their health to feed people and dealing with issues of racial inequity within both the workplace and the community. Ironically, some staff were having to use food pantries themselves. There was high staff turnover and a distinct lack of morale. People were given new job descriptions with no regard to their background, degree or experience. Employees were at their wits end. 'You'd walk by people's desks and see tears streaming down their faces. Who could work in that environment?', Emily asked.

The unionisation efforts soon gained momentum. At that time – back in September 2019 – the food bank was extremely opposed to it. The leadership team initially hired a notorious anti-union law firm, terminated employees without union representation, spread misinformation and created a hostile workplace by threatening staff and amplifying anti-union voices.[13] Emily told me that Tanis Crosby, the current executive director, was supportive of the union. The food bank now offers a union orientation with every new member of staff. 'People have taken this job *because* of the union', Emily told me.

Organisations from multiple states have reached out to hear more about the process of unionising. In November 2023, workers at the Alameda County food bank in California voted to unionise, with over 80 per cent voting in favour.[14] Workers across a range of positions, from warehouse associates to programme coordinators, hope that unionising will improve equity as well as increase pay and solidarity among staff. 'We see ourselves all serving one goal: to end hunger in the community', said Aila Dinglasan, programme coordinator at the food bank who I met during my visit to East Oakland. 'We're coming together to show that solidarity exists within our internal community, too.'

In 2013, a group of volunteers in Canada came together to form Freedom 90, the Union of Food Bank and Emergency Meal Program Volunteers. As a collective, they demanded an end to poverty and the need for food banks and emergency meal programmes in Ontario. Their charter emphasised that many volunteers at food banks and charitable food aid programmes are older women with wider caring responsibilities, as well as their own health and well-being, to consider. They had three core demands:

1. *Lay us off!* The Government of Ontario must ensure that social assistance and minimum wage levels are sufficient for everyone to have adequate housing and to buy their own food.

2. *Mandatory retirement by the age of 90!* Many of us have been volunteering for twenty years and there is no end in sight. The Freedom 90 Union demands the Government of Ontario take urgent action to end poverty and make food banks and emergency meal programs unnecessary.

3. *Freeze our wages! Or double them!* It doesn't matter because we are unpaid volunteers.[15]

Their website no longer exists, and despite their best efforts charitable food aid has continued to grow and institutionalise. I couldn't find out if the volunteers were able to retire before reaching the age of 90.

Wider issues around job precarity for food bank workers has been a key issue in Closing the Hunger Gap's 'Next Shift' campaign. Closing the Hunger Gap is a network of organisations and individuals working to expand hunger relief efforts beyond food distribution towards strategies that promote social justice and address the root causes of hunger. Their 'Next Shift' campaign urges charitable food organisations to pay 'thriving' wages and ensure fair, safe working conditions for all staff and workers. A thriving wage goes beyond the concept of a living wage, and includes realistic workloads, equitable pay and open communication without fear of retribution. As their narrative change campaign toolkit makes clear:

We know hard work isn't the problem – compensation and rampant unchecked capitalism is the problem. Racism, hunger, and economic exploitation are inextricably connected to each other as products of white supremacy and extractive capitalism. Organizations that claim to be working to end hunger that don't provide adequate wages and force their staff to decide between their personal safety and a paycheck is the problem.[16]

As I've written with colleagues elsewhere, it's important to recognise the underlying tensions in maintaining the current dominant model of charitable food aid that volunteers and workers face every day:

> Charitable food aid workers are concerned with meeting needs in their communities. They are not motivated by the expansion of corporate power, increased control over the food system and its profits. Indeed, many emergency food volunteers are themselves in situations of economic precarity. By working to recover surplus food as hunger relief, however, those working in food banks and their local network of partners have become instruments of a corporate food regime that promises to resolve two intractable problems born out of the profit driven food system – unsustainable overproduction and endemic hunger.[17]

Acknowledging these underlying tensions is vital, as charitable food aid workers, while striving to address community needs, often find themselves inadvertently entangled in a corporate food regime that prioritises profit over genuine solutions to both overproduction and hunger.

OBSTACLES TO ADVOCATING FOR CHANGE

To tackle these pressing challenges, it's essential that those working on the front lines of charitable food aid networks unite and collaboratively develop strategies. For many such individuals, finding the time and resources to engage in such initiatives can be incredibly difficult. The mounting pressure of meeting needs often leaves little room for planning and advocacy, making it all the more crucial that they can draw on support and solidarity. Staff and volunteers need to be responsive to an environment that changes every day. How much and what types of food will arrive? Will it be in a decent condition? Who will arrive to receive it, and how many people? What issues will they be dealing with? All these factors can make it difficult, if not impossible, for advocacy work to take place.

I visited many organisations who were aiming to do both, like Nourish East End mentioned in Chapter 4. Many of the food bank's volunteers also relied on it to support themselves, highlight-ing the precariousness and deep poverty in their own lives. Prior to my visit, I'd been in contact with Reverend Robin Wardlaw, who served on the board and as a regular Wednesday morning volun-teer. He retired as a minister several years ago from the church that houses the food bank and 'remains active in the fight for real food security as a volunteer'.

Over email ahead of my visit, Robin and I discussed a proposed trial of offering pre-loaded credit cards instead of groceries for some clients at Nourish. Although Robin was aware there would be benefits of such a trial, costs would also grow – he estimated it would increase their overall budget by three to five times. They might not be able to secure funding to run the pilot, but they were all deeply motivated to offer food in a different way. 'The limits of the charity model are on stark display', Robin stressed. He told me that he and the others on the board were interested in meeting with me to discuss how to 'shift the paradigm away from about-to-expire groceries in church basements'. Their proposed White Paper for the pilot stressed:

> Food banks have long been instrumental in addressing imme-diate hunger and providing emergency relief to those in need. However, there is a growing consensus that the current model of distributing perishable and non-perishable goods may not be the most efficient or dignified solution. This argument advo-cates for dismantling traditional food banks and replacing them with a system that prioritizes grocery cards, aiming for a more sustainable, client-centered, and empowering approach.[18]

Before arranging a meeting to discuss this further, I wanted to visit the food bank in person. I arrived at 8 am and there was already a handful of people waiting, although the food bank didn't open until 9 am. Robin explained they had introduced a lottery system, as previously people would start waiting at 6.30 am in the bitter cold: 'We were worried someone would freeze to death.'

Robin shared that the food bank has tripled in size over the past decade and now serves over 300 households each week. Some volunteers feel it has 'lost its cosy, friendly flavour', but as Robin pointed out, 'who has the time to stop and chat now?' The volunteers work with 100 people every hour. 'We really began to professionalise it the last four or five years', Robin added, noting that demand has continued to grow. Like many other organisations I visited, the boom and bust nature of the funding available during the pandemic also affected Nourish East End food bank. 'The money stopped cold' after the pandemic, Robin said, despite the ongoing need.

It turned out several volunteers hadn't showed up for their shift, so Robin asked if I could help out (I'd offered to volunteer when I first got in touch). I was assigned to the fruit and vegetables table by bustling volunteer coordinator Cathy, where I was stationed between two volunteers, one of whom uses the food bank himself. The table in front of us was loaded with potatoes, carrots, cabbages, oranges, apples, yellow zucchini (courgette) and Peruvian cucumbers. A lot of people didn't know what the yellow zucchini was, and we had a few laughs about the sheer size (and shape) of them. Like many of my volunteering experiences, it turned out to be busy and full-on, with not a lot of time to chat.

Afterwards, Robin had arranged for me to sit down with the other volunteers so I could hear more about their experiences. Volunteer Lea explained that for her, 'working in a food bank gives you a sense of self-esteem. For me, that's a really important thing'. The care and love that Lea and the others embodied in their roles was obvious. They really wanted to know what I thought of their food bank from my outsider perspective. Lea described how it's 'important to try and learn people's names'. Another piece of advice for a successful food bank encounter was, 'Don't rush – everyone is on edge to begin with'.

Robin said that it's important Lea is at the entrance, as she sets the tone. She's the most welcoming, gracious and patient. Its clear this meant a great deal to Lea as she shyly accepted Robin's compliments. The food bank hosts a volunteer appreciation night where people received framed certificates, which 'means a lot to our volunteers'. Volunteers can also receive an extra CAD$100 a month for volunteering after they've been there for two months, which is especially helpful for those who use the food bank themselves.

The conversation turned to food banking in general in Canada and the UK. 'We are institutionalised', Robin said. Reverend Breanne agreed. 'It's a 40-year emergency.' I asked what the food bank could be in the future – is there an exit strategy? '"Nourish" can mean lots of things', Robin said. 'We're really thinking about what transitioning to what "not a food bank" can look like. We've become part of the community now', Robin continued. 'If we can get rid of food banks, we become this social club.' We also talked about the need to get younger people involved – to do advocacy work, to do the heavy lifting – as many of the volunteers are mostly of retirement age, reminding me of the demands that Freedom 90 were making over ten years ago.

We reflected on the difficulties of managing scarcity and the expectations of people coming to the food bank. 'It's a moral injury to volunteers when they have to let customers know they can only have two oranges instead of three', Robin told me. 'I'm being abused for giving away free food', he continued. In the UK, Carl Walker and colleagues have explored how staff and volunteers manage hunger trauma in community food support organisations. They argue that moral injury is strongly linked to the idea of systemic betrayal:

> We found evidence of a sector where the feeling of being betrayed by a broader economic and political system was pronounced, as was the way that many volunteers felt that it was their responsibility, as moral citizens, to intervene in the sometimes overwhelming humiliation, trauma and distress that many in poverty encounter.[19]

As a result, those working on the front lines 'felt helpless and responsible for decisions which could negatively impact some of the most vulnerable people in society, and with little training or support available found themselves prone to emotional burnout, guilt, shame and distress which often stayed with them long after they left their shift'.

The charitable food aid system requires both physical labour – sourcing, sorting, packing and distributing food – and emotional care in terms of maintaining dignity, supporting people experiencing poverty and food insecurity, and fostering community trust and solidarity. It operates on the goodwill of volunteers and the dedicated efforts of staff, and it requires careful coordination to ensure food aid is delivered equitably, safely and with empathy. There is relentless skill and persistence involved in maintaining and negotiating complex relationships with donors, with charities and with people who are seeking support. Alongside all of this work, there is the invisible labour that goes on behind the scenes. The emotional strain and burnout of knowing that what you are offering is not a long-term solution – it's at best a temporary fix – weighs heavy on the people who are propping this inefficient and insufficient system up. From my own experiences as a volunteer throughout the last few years, the physical exertion is overtaken by the emotional work and care, which involves discretion and difficult decision making. Yet I've seen over the last few years of research that within all of this work – and when time and energies permit it – people on the front lines are mobilising and collectively advocating for structural change in reimagining what a future without food banks and food charity might look like.

PART II

Dignity, Rights and Solidarity

5

The Right to Food

THE RIGHT TO FOOD: THE MOST VIOLATED
HUMAN RIGHT WORLDWIDE?

What does the right to food mean to you? If you're reading this book, you're likely familiar with food banks and related forms of charitable food aid provision, but maybe the right to food is a lesser known concept. In fact, in their right to food explainer, Katie Boyle and Aidan Flegg state that: 'Often overlooked, the right to food provides a very clear example of the fact human rights violations are commonplace in rich, developed nations.'[1]

The right to food was first recognised in the 1948 Universal Declaration of Human Rights as part of the right to an adequate standard of living. This right was enshrined in the 1966 International Covenant on Economic, Social and Cultural Rights, which is an international treaty that aims to ensure the protection of economic, social and cultural rights, such as the rights to work, social security, health and education. Ten years later, in 1976, many countries signed the UN Covenant on Economic, Social and Cultural Rights (ICESCR), accepting a legal responsibility to respect, protect and fulfil the right to food.

Article 11(1) of the treaty recognises the right of everyone to an adequate standard of living, including adequate food, clothing and housing, and the continuous improvement of living conditions. Article 11(2) guarantees the fundamental right of everyone to be free from hunger, and obliges state parties (i.e. those countries that have voluntarily agreed to be bound by the treaty) to take steps in this regard, including the improvement of food distribution methods and dissemination of knowledge concerning nutrition. The UN Committee on Economic, Social and Cultural Rights (the body in charge of monitoring implementation of the ICESCR), declared that 'the right to adequate food is realized when every man, woman and child, alone or in community with others, has physical and economic access at all times to adequate food or means for its procurement'.[2]

The right to food definition can be broken down into several key elements, as defined by the UN Human Rights Office of the High Commissioner (OHCHR):

Availability – enough food should be produced for both present and future generations, acknowledging the notions of sustainability, or long-term availability, and the protection of the environment. Food should be available for sale in markets and shops.

Accessibility – food must be affordable. People should be able to afford food for an adequate diet without compromising any other basic needs, such as school fees, medicines or rent. Physical accessibility means food should be accessible to all, including people who are physically vulnerable.

Adequacy – the dietary needs of an individual must be fulfilled not only in terms of quantity but of nutritious quality. Food must satisfy dietary needs and be culturally acceptable.[3]

The right to food is therefore realised when all individuals, groups and communities are free from hunger and malnutrition, having gained constant physical and economic access to adequate food in a dignified, culturally acceptable and sustainable manner.

Although accessibility and affordability are often conflated in discussions about realising the right to food, they refer to different aspects of food security. Accessibility relates to the physical availability of food and the ability to obtain it, encompassing such factors as transportation and infrastructure. For example, a community might have a supermarket, but if people lack transportation or the food is not culturally appropriate, they may not be able to access it effectively. Affordability, meanwhile, refers to the economic aspect of food access – whether individuals can afford to purchase enough food to meet their nutritional needs. Even if food is physically accessible, it may still be unaffordable.

A total of 171 countries signed the treaty and are therefore legally bound by the ICESCR, including the right to adequate food. This means governments are legally required to secure the human right to adequate food for everyone. In November 2004, after two years of negotiation and consultation, the FAO adopted the Voluntary Right to Food Guidelines. Initiated by civil society, negotiated in a collaborative process and unanimously adopted by all FAO member states, the Right to Food Guidelines provided hope for a greater consensus on what states must do to fulfil their obligations under ICESCR.

The United States remains one of only four UN member states yet to ratify the covenant, and while the UK, Canada, Italy and 168 other countries have signed the treaty binding them to the ICESCR, this right to food language has not been weaved into their constitutions and legal mechanisms. In recent years, we've seen large increases in the levels of malnutrition, hunger and food bank usage, all of which are indicative of countries being in breach of their international legal obligations. As a consequence, dependence on the corporate capture of food charity to address poverty – not publicly funded, income-based solutions – has become the normalised and failed response.

ENSHRINING THE RIGHT TO FOOD IN LAW

Using international human rights law to assert the right to food remains a contentious matter in certain countries and regions. Canada, the US and the EU claim the right to food is not justiciable. In 2021, the US and Israel were the only countries to vote against a UN committee's draft that asserted food as a human right.[4] Without incorporating the right to food into domestic law, there are limited democratic mechanisms to challenge policies that cause persistent household food insecurity. In November 2022, Michael Fakhri, the UN special rapporteur on the right to food, explained to an Environment, Food and Rural Affairs (EFRA) Select Committee: 'The fact that a country like the United Kingdom has a developed welfare system means that you are not starting from zero. You have mechanisms that can be advanced. Defining the right to food means that everyone is entitled to their food always being adequate, available and accessible.'[5]

Given the scale of the growing poverty crisis in the UK and across rich-but-unequal countries, incorporating the right to food into domestic law offers a means of guaranteeing social protections and addressing the structural root causes of poverty. But as those working on the frontlines in charitable food and food justice organisations know, day-to-day need is ever increasing. Top-down policies such as a right to food can appear idealistic and unrealistic. It's also important not to isolate the right to food from the other socio-economic rights in the ICESCR, such as the right to work, right to health or right to social security. Ultimately, addressing food insecurity through the lens of structural inequality demands an integrated approach which acknowledges that interconnected rights are essential for fostering an equitable society where the right to food can be realised.

In the US, there is a growing movement towards embedding a right to food in state constitutions. In 2021, voters in Maine, Massachusetts approved a constitutional amendment guaranteeing a 'natural, inherent and unalienable right' to food.[6] The same year, a US National Right to Food Community of Practice (CoP) was formed to bring together advocates, legal experts, community organisers, food and farm organisations, small-scale food producers and those with lived experience of hunger,[7] thereby building capacity among state-level organisers and community-based organisations advocating for the right to food. In February 2024, Director of the CoP Alison Cohen told me:

A strong reason why the CoP came about is because of Maine's long road but ultimate success in changing their constitution to include food as a human right. The first in our nation. And also part of what fuelled the coalition was Trump's election to the presidency. Among food and farm advocates and organisers, there was just this incredible feeling that 'Nothing's gonna happen at federal level'. Nothing good is gonna happen there, or nothing transformational, let me put it that way. And as Eleanor Roosevelt said, the right to food will be realised in places close to home. And I think that's true. We saw it happen in Maine. Maine was very particular, a very strong ideology around libertarianism with a still strong tradition of small farmers organising around local food sovereignty. All of which I think was really instrumental in passing the right to food constitutional amendment.

Picking up on the quote Alison referred to by Eleanor Roosevelt, it states that we must start the fight for universal rights in 'small places, close to home':

> Where, after all, do universal human rights begin? In small places, close to home – so close and so small that they cannot be seen on any maps of the world … Such are the places where every man, woman, and child seeks equal justice, equal opportunity, equal dignity without discrimination. Unless these rights have meaning there, they have little meaning anywhere. Without concerted citizen action to uphold them close to home, we shall look in vain for progress in the larger world.[8]

This emphasis on grassroots, community-based action resonates with the growing momentum for the right to food in the UK and across Europe. In the UK, there are several 'right to food cities', the first being Liverpool in January 2021. The UK Right to Food campaign is being led by Labour MP Ian Byrne from Liverpool West Derby,[9] in collaboration with the grassroots initiative Fans Supporting Foodbanks. Supported by organisations such as Amnesty International and Human Rights Watch, the campaign has five main goals: universal free school meals for every child; a government commitment to specifying how much of minimum wages and benefits should go towards food; independent enforcement of right to food legislation; the establishment of community kitchens; and ensuring food security for all.

Pledging to eradicate household food insecurity in a dignified and sustainable way, UK Right to Food cities and towns now include Birmingham, Brighton and Hove, Cumberland, Durham, Hackney, Lancaster, Liverpool, Manchester, Newcastle, Rotherham, Sheffield and Southampton. I asked Ian about what the right to food could achieve, and he told me:

> If you want to build a society which we all want, because you hear a lot of talk about productivity, you hear a lot of talk about

economic growth, but it won't come from a sick, hungry nation, will it? It just won't. You know, it's an impossible task. You've got to solve poverty. You've got to solve the systemic failings which are holding people back. And there's so many elements to that. But for me, poverty is the major number one issue which should be resolved, and then from that, you'll get a far more equitable and healthy society. So we put right to food right at the heart of that conversation.

A developing right to food movement is also spreading across countries in Europe. In June 2023, Geneva became the first Swiss canton to solidify the right to food in its constitution after a popular vote. The same month, the Scottish government became the first in the world to publish a plan entitled 'Cash-First: Towards Ending the Need for Food Banks in Scotland', which set out a human rights approach to tackling food insecurity and ending the need for food banks.[10] Meanwhile, the German Ministry of Food and Agriculture established a stand-alone division in 2023 dedicated to the right to food. Ahead of the 20th anniversary of the Right to Food Guidelines in 2024, the European Citizens Initiative called on the European Commission to ensure dignified access to sufficient, healthy and sustainable food for all.[11]

I wanted to capture the momentum building around the right to food in recent years. In the US, I intentionally visited states working to enshrine the right to food in their constitutions, including California, Washington and West Virginia. I sought out right to food cities in the UK, including Birmingham, Durham and Newcastle, to see what this means in practice. In Europe, I visited the Basque Country, Belgium and Italy to understand how movements are working towards realising the right to food on the ground, and the challenges and opportunities involved.

WHAT CAN REALISING A RIGHT TO FOOD MEAN IN PRACTICE?

The guiding principles of the right to food were often mentioned to me when visiting food justice organisations, food banks and pantries, social services departments and food policy councils, but they were trickier to operationalise in practice. I found that despite often being an organisational goal, it was not universally adopted in communications. Andy Fisher, long-time community activist and author of *Big Hunger*, explains why this could be from a US perspective: 'Because the rights framework has proven so politically problematic in the short-term, anti-hunger groups have instead chosen to employ language based on the moral imperative of ending hunger. They focus on food as a human need rather than as a human right.'

Speaking to Michael Fakhri, the UN Special Rapporteur for the Right to Food and Nutrition in May 2023 on my visit to Oregon state, he agreed, telling me, 'food is a human right' speaks to Americans more than a 'right to food'.

Some Latin American countries provide examples of how the right to food can be operationalised. Bolivia, Cuba, Mexico and Brazil have all incorporated the right to food into their respective constitutions, with Brazil regarded as a success story of how the right to food can be implemented on the ground. Belo Horizonte, Brazil's fourth largest city, was deemed to be 'the city that ended hunger'.[12] Developed in 1993 to address food and nutrition security in the city, Belo Horizonte's approach to food security was one of the first integrated food security policies to be developed in the world. By implementing a mix of policy and market strategies, alongside engaging the community, the city successfully reached about 40 per cent of its 2.5 million residents, halving the rate of infant mortality over a decade.

Specifically, the city facilitated connections between local farmers and consumers by creating farmers' markets, employed pricing strategies to make certain fruits and vegetables more accessible, and launched Restaurante Popular, or People's Restaurants, to provide affordable, nutritious meals. Part of their approach included the institutionalisation of the right to food at the federal level, leading to supportive policy frameworks. Additional initiatives targeted community and school gardens, as well as nutrition education. These efforts were rooted in the belief that having access to quality food is a fundamental human right.

Saulo Arantes Ceolin and Luiz Carlos Keppe Nogueira from the Ministry of Foreign Affairs of Brazil have explained how, from the 2000s, the Brazilian government rolled out a series of strategic policies promoting food security and nutrition.[13] Between 2004 and 2013, targeted policies to eradicate poverty, such as universal free school meals, helped cut the rate of Brazilian households facing hunger from 9.5 per cent to 4.2 per cent. The success of these policies even led to Brazil's removal from the FAO's Hunger Map in 2014 and established the nation as a global benchmark in the promotion of the right to food. The pandemic, however, led to rocketing food insecurity rates, with children unable to go to school to access their free school meals. Right-wing populist President Jair Bolsonaro introduced austerity measures that systematically dismantled the foundations of food and nutrition security policies just before the pandemic, leading to a perfect storm of soaring unemployment, homelessness and hunger.

Brazil's case shows not only the importance of joined up, government-backed policies to tackle poverty but also the fragility of their success. One of the main objectives of current Brazilian President Luiz Inácio Lula da Silva is to strengthen the public policies that made Brazil a shining example worldwide. Breaking down in tears following his election, Lula said: 'If at the end of my term in 2026, every Brazilian is having breakfast, lunch and dinner once again, I will have fulfilled my life's mission.'[14] In August 2023, Lula announced Brasil Sem Fome, the Brazil Without Hunger plan, a series of measures to help combat the hunger that had returned to the country. They included boosting incomes through an updated social welfare programme, increasing the national minimum wage, and emphasising the importance of the universal free school meals programme. Brasil Sem Fome was described by Professor Elisabetta Recine, president of the Council for Food and Nutrition Security of Brazil, as 'arguably the most comprehensive set of anti-hunger policies the world has ever seen',[15] offering hope where hope is lacking.

WHY WE SHOULD THINK ABOUT RIGHTS, NOT CHARITY

Food charity is not a right – it cannot be claimed. Activists, NGOs and academics have long called for a separation of rights and charity. As Professor Hilal Elver, former UN special rapporteur on the right to food, explains:

> It needs to be clarified that there is a fundamental difference between charity and the right to food. Charity is a voluntary commitment. In contrast, the right to food is a legal entitlement of individuals that places on UN member states the obligation to create and maintain adequate human rights institutions and avenues, so that rights holders can hold them accountable for violations of their right to food, and secure remedial relief for themselves.[16]

Professor Graham Riches, author of *Food Bank Nations*, has been researching poverty, food charity and the right to food in Canada and the Global North since the 1980s. Even after retirement, Graham continues to be an active member of the GSA collective. In February 2024, I asked him what realising the right to food might look like in practice:

> It's about meeting a basic human need, living wages, adequate social security and a fully funded welfare state. If UK history is any guide you have this potential. After all, you have *The Guardian* and all those people who think critically about food and social policy. Certainly, the right to food isn't only about income. It's also about growing, hunting, gathering, distributing healthy and nutritious food and learning from the food sovereignty movement. It's about choice, equity, and dignity, being able to feed yourself and your families. Essentially, it's seeing the state as the primary duty bearer and the critical role played by all as rights holders in civil society holding governments to account for their right to food obligations under international law.

As Graham acknowledges, the right to food is about more than just someone being able to access food. It's about taste, enjoyment, connection, culture and heritage. A potential drawback of the right to food, then, is the perception of it as a legalistic, top-down idea that focuses on the state as the main duty bearer. This can sideline the power and solidarity found in communities and their role in ensuring people can access good quality, culturally relevant and nutritious food. This is where the framework of food sovereignty can helpfully be used to map out how we address the power inequalities characteristic of the global food system.

This book isn't saying that food banks and charitable food aid are 'bad'. Right now, they're one of the only ways that people on a low income are able to feed themselves and their families – *temporarily*. But charitable food aid shouldn't be seen as a solution to poverty and inequality. Almost everybody I met throughout my visits – food bank CEOs, volunteers, social workers, people working in NGOs, people using charitable food aid sites – agreed that receiving food in this way is at best a passing relief and at worst an undignified, inadequate solution. We have known this for decades, and yet the charitable food aid model continues to be backed by billion dollar companies and touted as a solution to hunger by organisations such as the GFN. In drawing attention to the rapidly growing institutionalisation and corporate involvement in charitable food aid, this book encourages readers to think about the tensions and challenges of charitable food aid in meeting people's basic needs, and instead consider alternatives based on rights and solidarity within communities.

6

Reducing Stigma, Promoting Dignity, Nurturing Solidarity

Being able to feed yourself and your family food that is culturally relevant, that you've chosen and that you've accessed through
dignified means – whether growing your own or having adequate
income to purchase it – are fundamental prerequisites to the right
to food. Research – including my own[1] – tells us that the stigma
so often associated with accessing charitable food aid can leave
people feeling judged, othered and undeserving.

As I've written with colleagues Charlie Spring and Andy Fisher,
'charity remains a vector of othering, while poverty induces shame
that can prevent people from seeking assistance or engaging politically to demand their rights to basic needs security'.[2] Rebecca de
Souza, author of *Feeding the Other: Whiteness, Privilege, and Neoliberal Stigma in Food Pantries*, talks about the deeply entrenched
neoliberal stigma of food pantries in the US, explaining how it is
heavily racialised, gendered and classed.[3] This leads to an unequal
experience of food insecurity in charitable food aid settings. Similarly, in her research on US food banking, Alana Haynes Stein
found that 'inequitable practices and interactions persist in food
assistance programs, as the staff, volunteers, and funders of food
banks generally occupy different classed, racialized, and gendered
positions than food bank clients'.[4] These power dynamics –
between volunteers, workers, and receivers – can also be found
among people receiving charitable food aid themselves.

Across the 90 or more organisations I visited between May 2022
and November 2024, it was hard to find an organisation that *didn't*
prioritise dignity and choice – at least on paper. In reality, especially when I was volunteering, I found it was incredibly difficult,
if not impossible, to offer a truly dignified experience for people
experiencing food insecurity and seeking help.

HOW WE TALK ABOUT CHARITABLE
FOOD AID MATTERS

In my 2016 book *Hunger Pains*, I dedicated an entire chapter to the politics of food bank use in the UK, noting how government explanations for rising food bank use tended to focus on individualised behaviour, specifically poor financial management, smoking, drinking alcohol, drug taking and spending money on tattoos, satellite television and dogs. These narratives still exist, despite a lack of evidence to back up claims of rising food bank use as a consequence of lazy, uneducated people who use a food bank simply because it's there. For example, in May 2022, Lee Anderson MP claimed that food banks are largely unnecessary because the main cause of food poverty is a lack of cooking and budgetary skills – and that nutritious meals could be easily cooked for 30 pence a time. 'We've got generation after generation who cannot cook properly, they can't cook a meal from scratch, they cannot budget', he said. 'I think you'll see first-hand there's not this massive use for food banks in this country.'[5] While such judgements are less common than when I was writing *Hunger Pains* nearly a decade ago, they persist, reflecting a continued tendency to blame individuals for structural failures.

Alongside stereotypical judgements that reinforce systemic inequalities, there is a celebratory narrative that portrays those who donate and volunteer at charitable food aid sites as 'heroes' and 'angels'. National Food Bank Day is celebrated on the first Friday of September in the US and, more recently, in the UK to 'recognise the incredible work of food banks, volunteers, businesses, and organisations that are dedicated to fighting hunger and making a difference to the lives of those in need'.[6] In 2023, the GFN encouraged website visitors to send a personalised message of thanks to a specific food bank. The campaign urged:

We want to make sure these exceptional people around the world don't go unnoticed, so we're *Celebrating the Faces of Food Banking*. These are the people who make food banks and hunger alleviation around the world possible – from those harvesting

produce on the farm to those serving up a hot meal or distributing parcels of food to those who need it most.[7]

It's important to move beyond a framing that paints those seeking
charitable food aid as passive recipients, which perpetuates false
narratives that people experiencing poverty will always be with
us and need charity as a response. Reclaiming the conversation
around poverty and food insecurity has become a key goal for
many narrative change campaigns, including my own work with
the GSA.

The GSA, alongside other networks such as the National Right to
Food CoP in the US, provide platforms where food bank workers,
volunteers and recipients can use narrative change as a tool for
transformation. One standout example is the Next Shift campaign,[8]
born out of Closing the Hunger Gap in the US, which incorporates strategies for social justice and addressing the root causes of
hunger and poverty. In all these spaces, charitable food aid workers
and volunteers are integral to the conversation, united by a shared
commitment to creating a just food system that upholds everyone's
right to food and dignity.

True narrative change requires more than just participation –
it demands a shift in who gets to tell the story. A significant part
of reframing the discourse around charitable food aid involves
ensuring people with lived experience of poverty and food insecurity are part of the conversation. In rural, underresourced West
Virginia (WV), Voices of Hunger is a collective of anti-hunger
activists, food system development practitioners, farmers and
lawmakers working to break the cycles of poverty exacerbating
household food insecurity by humanising the experience of hunger
through personal storytelling.[9] Envisioned as a means of breaking
the 'silent violence of hunger' and encouraging those with lived
experiences to share their stories among peers, Voices of Hunger
WV convene monthly public virtual meetings and engage participants in conversation, pedagogy and action around advancing the
right to food. Made up by a cohort of community-based organisers, they've experimented with fellowships, which pay a stipend of
$500 to encourage people to come together and learn about the
potential of a right to food.

I was invited to a hybrid meeting of Voices of Hunger WV in October 2022. It was their first in-person gathering, as they initially formed during the pandemic, and took place in a small library just off the highway, with the library cat in attendance. The fact the meeting was held here was not accidental. The decision was made to ensure meetings are held in accessible public spaces that foster participation and diminish uneven power dynamics. During the meeting, there was a lot of discussion about how we can tell stories effectively – both to share information between peers and effect change. To that end, the group has already seen success. In 2022, Morgantown city council passed a municipal resolution on the Right to Food, and there are emergent initiatives in other cities and counties that may now follow suit. The collective hope of Voices of Hunger WV is to enshrine the right to food in the West Virginia Constitution. But ongoing tensions in trying to fairly compensate people for this type of work, with little to no funding, restrict what the group is able to do. Josh Lohnes, one of the co-founders, said to me: 'How do you compensate someone fairly for their time, when that compensation might lead to them losing their SNAP benefits? But there are not actually sufficient resources to compensate people full time to do advocacy or community food work.'

Voices of Hunger WV has received some additional support to continue organising and has another round of fellows (some returning), each of whom has received a $500 stipend to assist them in advancing whatever project they deem might 'seed sparks' for the right to food. Josh continued: 'The challenge is to continue to support the many different people that have contributed to this project, in the midst of "advocacy burnout" and household economic precarity, while meaningfully building a movement that changes the way we all relate to food and hunger work.'

Other campaigns are specifically homing in on policy change, such as advocating for a universal basic income (UBI). As the Joseph Rowntree Foundation have explained, models of UBI differ, but the basic premise is that every individual receives an unconditional regular cash payment without reference to their other income or wealth.[10] Payment amounts vary depending on demographic characteristics, such as a different payment for work-ing-age adults, children and pensioners. The idea has been tested in countries such as Finland, Canada and Wales but has not been continued in any context, largely due to the costs associated with it.[11] This is despite the proven benefits of UBI, including improved mental and physical health.[12]

Matt Noble, founder and executive director of the Toronto Vegetarian Food Bank in Canada, launched the 'Put Food Banks Out of Business' campaign in October 2024, advocating for a guaranteed liveable basic income as a solution to end the need for food banks altogether.[13] The Toronto Vegetarian Food Bank is a vegan food bank that has provided over 350,000 meals worth of fresh, nutritious, plant-based groceries to community members facing poverty and food insecurity since its inception in 2015. I had hoped to visit the food bank during my trip, but it only operates as a once-a-month pop-up, so instead I met Matt for lunch at Gia, a plant-based restaurant in the Dundas West area of the city.

'I never intended for this to be my job', Matt explained, reflecting on how the pandemic shifted his focus to running the food bank and engaging in food policy and advocacy full time. He started the food bank in his spare time, driven by necessity. At the time, he was designing high-end custom kitchens but came to realise his work was contributing to a larger issue – the rising cost of housing, which was already out of reach for many Canadians. He is passionate that 'poor people shouldn't be dumpsters for rubbish food', so the food bank allocates 50–60 per cent of its budget to fresh fruits and vegetables. 'We don't want people to have to compromise their health or their ethics when they're already in such a vulnerable position', he added. The 'Put Food Banks Out of Business' campaign demands focus on ensuring everyone has enough money to ensure their basic needs are met. Matt told me: 'Poverty is expensive. It ends up costing us all more in extra healthcare spending, mental health support, policy, prisons, and costly emergency shelter and support services.'

The campaign is calling on all levels of government to collaborate on implementing a guaranteed liveable basic income, ensuring that no one in Canada is left below the poverty line. 'UBI is the most effective way to address poverty from a policy standpoint. It's essentially a solution to eliminate poverty', Matt explained. 'Hunger doesn't wait for policy change.' According to statistics from PROOF, a research programme at the University of Toronto that studies household food insecurity in Canada and develops evidence-based policy solutions to reduce it, nearly two in five Black and Indigenous people in Canada live in households facing food insecurity.[14] A basic income could play a crucial role in tackling the deep-rooted issues of systemic racism and income inequality. As I've written with colleagues elsewhere, the pandemic has led to a questioning of the current, ineffective status quo: 'In this time of reckoning with systems of economic exploitation based on colonialism, patriarchy, misogyny, anti-Black racism, capitalist accumulation and ableism, demands have resurfaced that basic needs to be met not by well-meaning volunteers, but by universal income and service guarantees.'[15]

Matt was vocal about the tensions between trying to ensure more dignity through alternatives such as shopping vouchers instead of people accessing a food bank. 'I've had to talk down loads of activists about giving out vouchers.' I asked what he meant. 'Vouchers can take away that paternalism, but they're still rooted in the ideology that food is the problem. Also, its much more dignified going into a store and spending money, not vouchers.'

This highlights a dilemma that has surfaced in every city I've visited, whether in the US, Europe or Canada. Should the focus be on improving the current charitable food aid system – by creating more welcoming spaces, offering healthier options and providing more choice? Or should we shift our energy towards advocating for policies such as UBI that could address food insecurity at its root? With the rise of social pantries, community kitchens, town fridges and food clubs, can we achieve both – improving the system and addressing the root causes?

'IT SHOULD LOOK LIKE A STORE, NOT A FOOD BANK'

A unifying theme across many organisations I visited was around the importance of how a space *felt*. Not just what it looked like aesthetically, but how it sounded, how it was presented and how it could be accessed. As Heide K. Bruckner and colleagues point out, 'how free food *feels* can either support or inhibit food justice goals.'[16]

The SODO Community Market, provided by Northwest Harvest in Seattle, is a prime example of this philosophy in action. It was intentionally designed to create a dignified shopping experience rather than the stigmatising atmosphere typically associated with food banks. To better understand how the market operated, I arranged to volunteer on a Wednesday morning. I arrived just after 7 am to pick up my badge and take part in the volunteer huddle where roles were assigned. I chose to be a 'floater', so I could assist shoppers, help with restocking and ensure the market stayed clean and organised. Shaun,[17] a staff member, gave us a brief tour and explained the market's rules – no policing of items, maintain stocked shelves and keep the space tidy.

I started by stocking cabbage, broccoli and asparagus, darting back and forth between the warehouse and the shopping area. While there were suggested limits for the amount of produce per shopper, such as one red pepper or one bunch of asparagus, few shoppers adhered strictly to these limits. One volunteer explained to me that people often cook for large families, so a single pepper or bunch of asparagus doesn't stretch very far. Despite Shaun's clear instruction not to police the shopping experience, I witnessed him reprimand several people quite sternly for taking more than the suggested amount. 'Think about other people!' he said, scolding shoppers for being 'greedy' and instructing them to put items back. Shortly after, I saw an older woman discreetly slip three red peppers into her shopping trolley. I didn't intervene but felt a pang of guilt when, later in the shift, the peppers and asparagus ran out completely.

When the market first opened, the shelves were full, offering a wide variety of produce. But as the shift wore on, supplies began to dwindle. By 10.30 am, the options were limited. A woman approached me, holding a few leftover asparagus tips and asking in broken English if there was any more. I checked with Shaun, who explained that we couldn't restock the shelves as there had to be enough for the second shift, which ran from 11 am to 2 pm. Volunteers informed shoppers they could return later and try again.

As the market began to slow down, long-time volunteer Jim suggested we check the warehouse for some different varieties of soup to offer more choice to shoppers. We brought out tins of New

England clam chowder, chicken noodle soup and bone broth to sit alongside the tomato soup already on the shelves. Soon after, Shaun pointed at the shelf. 'What's going on with the soup?' he asked. One of the other volunteers, who was stacking water and energy drinks nearby, gave me a disapproving look. I explained that I'd arranged the soups that way. Shaun shook his head. 'No. It should look like a store, not a food bank'. I offered to fix it, but he shrugged, 'It's done now'. People did take the different varieties of soup, but it admittedly looked messier than if all the cans of tomato soup had been lined up neatly. I felt like I'd done something wrong, so tried to rearrange the shelf, grouping similar items together and tidying it up, wondering – is it more dignified to offer more choice or to present a neater, more organised selection?

The physical space of charitable and community food aid is one that is constantly being negotiated and renegotiated. Architects are designing food banks and pantries to offer welcoming, comfortable and dignified spaces that mirror a 'normal' shopping experience. During the pandemic, organisations often had to resort to giving out pre-made boxes of food and closing off their social spaces where people could gather. This in turn meant the introduction of lengthy queues, a lack of interaction with volunteers and workers, and an experience that was far removed from what could be classed as a dignified experience. At the beginning of the research for this book, many organisations were still operating in this way. As time progressed, elements of choice were reintroduced and the social, community aspect of charitable food aid mostly returned. This included social eating and community meals, which are based on a menu of low-cost or free meals prepared using food surpluses and deliberately served communally to improve social inclusion and reduce loneliness.

One such example of the power of bringing people together to eat in a carefully designed, welcoming space can be found at a community dinner at the Refettorio at Farming Hope, a culinary job training and food justice non-profit in San Francisco's Tenderloin district. The Refettorio was established in conjunction with Michelin star chef Massimo Bottura's non-profit Food for Soul. A 'refettorio' is a community hub that serves free meals to people who need it, using surplus ingredients. The word itself comes from the Latin word *reficere*, which means 'to remake' or 'to restore'. The original purpose of a refettorio was for monks to share their daily meal. Today, refettorios are intended to create communities, prevent social isolation and fight food waste.

Once the Uber driver was satisfied I could be let out of the car in this neighbourhood as a woman on her own, I checked in with a smiling server at the door, just like in a restaurant. It had been a long day, so I was relieved that they were expecting me. While I was waiting for General Manager Ram Olivares-Ochoa to come and meet me, I had a good look around. The space was bright and vibrant and felt like a high-end restaurant. Starched white table-cloths covered the tables and glass vases of fresh yellow flowers were perched in the centre. Families were chatting, laughing and connecting – both with each other and the volunteers who were busily moving around the space. In front of me, there was an open kitchen with a large mirror positioned above the counter, reflecting the chefs as they prepared the meals. The stylish orange lighting created a welcoming ambience, far removed from the harsh fluorescent strip lights often found in charitable food aid spaces.

The kitchen offers more than just community meals. Farming Hope offers a twelve-week paid culinary training apprenticeship programme for people facing barriers to employment, including former incarceration, homelessness or long-term unemployment. Ram told me that the vast majority of apprentices go on to work in the food industry, in restaurants, grocery stores, commercial kitchens or food manufacturing. There are seven or eight volunteers at the community dinner serving around 80 people every week. The food is all surplus (or 'rescued food', as Ram called it), and each week the chefs devise a menu depending on what they've got. After a tour of the space, I sat down with Ram at a table with regulars Dave, his friend and her young daughter. There was a printed menu decorated with cheerful illustrations that told us what we would be eating tonight. 'I get as excited about the menu as I do the food', Dave told me.

Dave was also really excited that Ram, the manager, was sitting down to eat with him, and used the opportunity to share some of his ideas about the dinners. He asked Ram if they'd ever thought of doing themed nights that were culturally relevant, such as a

Mexican night, to reflect the diversity of people from the local community who come along to dine together each week. According to 2021 Census data, 43 per cent of the Tenderloin identifies as immigrants.[18] On the night of my visit, the first course was ham and parmigiano arancini served with white beans and rocket. The second course featured a minced beef Wellington with cabbage, followed by homemade chocolate chip cookies for dessert.

At the end of the meal, as the cookies were being served at each table, I noticed people starting to queue up and asked Ram what was happening. He explained that, in addition to the meal, everyone receives a bag of fresh produce to take home. Up until that point, anyone walking by would have assumed the meal was just like any other restaurant experience. But the act of queuing for surplus food subtly shifted the power dynamics that the volunteers were working to dismantle. Dave's friend asked for a takeaway container and ended up taking the entire plate of cookies home with her, also filling a flask with tea. While these small actions reminded me that we weren't in a high-end restaurant, the overall atmosphere was one of genuine community and connection. There was a warmth that extended beyond the physical space and made it feel far more lived-in than its two months of occupation would suggest.

Community meals such as those served at the Refettorio aim to foster solidarity by creating safe, inclusive spaces where people from diverse backgrounds can reconnect and find joy in food again. If we return to the concept of a right to food, it's about choice, dignity and accessibility. The meal we shared on that evening was about more than that. It was about enjoyment. It was the joy on Dave's face when he saw the menu, the excitement in the way the meals were presented and the experience of being served as in a good restaurant. The food was not only nutritious but also tasty and appealing, offering a real sense of care and attention to people experiencing food insecurity.

In this way, the Refettorio concept – and other forms of social eating – demonstrate how a dignified eating experience can be both a source of nourishment and connection. In the UK, Nourish Scotland have called for the introduction of public diners as a new piece of national infrastructure, underscoring the power of communal meals in fostering both physical and social well-being.[19] Linked to my experience in the refettorio in Tenderloin, their report emphasises:

> Food in a public diner doesn't have to be perfect, but it has to be good – and keep improving over time. Food isn't nutrition until it reaches the stomach. Taste is the key factor that keeps bringing people back to public diners, and in turn maximises the benefits that flow from them. Public diners escape the false dichotomy of taste vs health, serving delicious dishes which help people to stay nourished and well.[20]

As Dave pointed out, one way to improve the dining experience would be to diversify the types of food offered, ensuring they align with diners' cultural preferences. However, since the chefs are working with surplus food rather than selecting ingredients themselves, this isn't always feasible.

SOLIDARITY, NOT CHARITY

Mutual aid organisations offering food emphasise the creation of non-hierarchical, community-driven spaces where everyone is treated with respect and as equals. Unlike traditional charity models, mutual aid operates on the principle of solidarity rather than charity, with the aim of ensuring people receiving food are seen not as passive 'recipients' but as active participants in a supportive, inclusive community. Here, food sharing is a collective effort rather than an act of benevolence. Mutual aid organisations often work to radically reimagine local food systems using a food sovereignty lens.

La Via Campesina has been a leading force in promoting food sovereignty as an alternative to the more conventional food security framework, which typically focuses on ensuring all people have access to sufficient, safe and nutritious food to meet their dietary needs.[21] Founded in Belgium in 1993, this global movement unites millions of peasants, landless workers, Indigenous peoples, pastoralists, fishers, migrant farmworkers, small-scale farmers, rural women and youth from all corners of the world. Food sovereignty is defined as the right of people to healthy, culturally appropriate food produced using sustainable methods, based on the needs, desires and values of the people themselves.[22] Unlike the concept of food security, which has been criticised for being overly dependent on the industrialised global food system, food sovereignty centres on grassroots movements and highlights the importance of historical context, power dynamics and justice in food production and consumption.

Over the past three decades, La Via Campesina has secured a voice in global governance, participating at key institutions such as the FAO and the Civil Society and Indigenous Peoples' Mechanism within the Committee on World Food Security. This has led to a shift in how the right to food is understood by international bodies, with an increasing emphasis on food sovereignty. While food security tends to view hunger primarily as an issue of access to food, food sovereignty frames it as a question of power – specifically, who controls the resources that shape food production. Under this framework, hunger is not simply alleviated through charitable food aid but addressed at its roots by dismantling the systemic barriers perpetuating food insecurity.

Mutual aid and food sovereignty naturally align, as both prioritise community empowerment, self-determination and collective action. Mutual aid involves communities organising to meet their own needs, like sharing food, without relying on external authorities or systems. This directly complements food sovereignty's call for local control over food systems, allowing communities to produce, distribute and consume food in ways that are culturally relevant and environmentally sustainable. When traditional systems fail those who are marginalised by systemic injustice, mutual aid becomes a means for communities to act collectively and drive change. This spirit of solidarity, rather than charity, led me to the Chicagoland Food Sovereignty Coalition (CFSC). Formed in December 2020, this grassroots coalition brings together over 30 autonomous mutual aid groups working to reimagine a resilient, sustainable and equitable local food system based on food sovereignty principles and mutual aid practices. Their website emphasises:

This is an autonomous mutual aid network, not a state-based charity effort. We are here to share as equals in the rich experience of mutual aid. We are here to honor each other with consistent service, care, and collaboration. We are prioritizing and building momentum with folks who are sick, disabled, houseless, quarantined without income, economically disadvantaged, elderly, undocumented, incarcerated, detained, queer, Black, Indigenous, and/or people of color, or who have families in need.[23]

The aim of CFSC is to foster horizontal relationships without hierarchy. Their website is clear – they refuse to work with cops, white supremacists or misogynists, and they attempt to root out 'learned hierarchical tendencies' within the network.

I reached out to the CFSC twice and, on my second attempt, received a response from Bill Mengebier, a volunteer with both his local Mayfair Mutual Aid group and CFSC. Bill invited me to join him for a couple of 'food rescues' on Memorial Day in May 2024. He picked me up in the West Loop neighbourhood where I was staying, and we set off for two Aldi stores. Bill told me he joined CFSC in early 2021. He runs his own business and is 'almost' retired. On our drive through Wicker Park, Ukrainian Village and Logan Square en route to the Aldi stores and CFSC's warehouses, he explained their mission. CFSC is intentional about redistributing food and resources from the wealthier North Side – where there is 'more money, more privilege, more opportunity' – to the historically underserved South and West Sides of Chicago. Bill told me CFSC has around 30 core volunteers, with about 100 total if you include the broader network. Approximately 90 per cent of their volunteer time is dedicated to 'food rescue'. With 24 rescues happening every week, the logistics are labour-intensive. 'It's almost primitive', Bill said. Food is constantly moving between different places. To keep everything running smoothly, they have rotating food rescue coordinators, though this leaves little time for the movement-building work they initially set out to do.

'It's pretty rare we miss a rescue', Bill said as we drove to our first pick up of the day. The stores need to be able to rely on CFSC to pick up the food, and building strong relationships with store managers is crucial. 'They know we'll be there when we say we will', he explained. Three-quarters of the food they pick up is what Bill considers 'grocery store quality'. I saw that first hand on our rescues. When we arrived, there were bags of salad, tangerines, bananas, frozen bread, bagels and pizzas ready for pickup. The food was near its expiration date, but it would soon be redistributed to one of the many community fridges, called Love Fridges, or partner organisations in the coalition.

Bill emphasised the importance of giving people the ability to choose the food they want. 'If people can choose it, it's more palatable', he explained, speaking to the challenges of working with surplus food. Once we returned to CFSC's Keystone warehouse in the Hermosa neighbourhood, I helped unload the truck. Bill took photos of the food received to post on their Slack channel, letting everyone know what had arrived. He showed me how to use the pallet jack to move the food into the cooler, the freezers and dry storage shelves. It was tough work, but surprisingly, I was quite good at it!

Bill told me there is a huge demand for community fridges in the neighbourhoods CFSC serves. Chicago's Love Fridge mutual aid organisation is one example of mutual aid efforts that emerged during the pandemic. With a mission to reduce food waste and advocate for food as a right, not a privilege, Love Fridge aims to radically transform food systems and community safety. Operating under principles of reciprocal practice and collective care, Love Fridge seeks to address food apartheid on Chicago's South and West Sides, ensuring food access is equitable and continuous. The organisation has set up over 25 community fridges, each one painted by local artists to reflect the diverse neighbourhoods they serve. These fridges allow neighbours to donate food as well as take what they need, providing 24/7 access to fresh produce and essential staples.

Love Fridge has established clear guidelines on what can and cannot be donated. For example, they ask that people avoid donating raw meat and fish, packaged items not labelled with a use-by date, opened items, anything you would not consume yourself, half-eaten leftovers or alcohol. Running and maintaining community fridges isn't easy. The volunteers are putting food in, and at the same time people are pulling the food out. Outside their Keystone warehouse, there's a currently defunct community fridge which they had to take out of commission as the local neighbours were complaining. People hanging around the fridge was 'making people in the neighbourhood nervous', Bill said.

I heard similar stories about community fridges in Vancouver and Oakland, where high demand can lead to tensions between people using the fridges and local residents. It's a constant battle to make sure the fridges stay plugged in so that the food doesn't spoil. I was told how donors would leave expired food in and around the fridges, which led to yet more waste and could attract pests. This creates even more labour for volunteers taking care of the fridges. In an analysis of 20 community fridge Instagram accounts from the US and Canada, Constance Gordon found that: 'In numerous cases, the labor of sustaining – purchasing, transporting, distributing, stocking, cleaning, posting, responding, and more – falls on a small central collective or even just one person.'[24]

Rejecting charity and saviourism, the town fridges and mutual aid networks I visited were fuelled by kindness, reciprocal generosity and collective care. However, the expectation of reciprocity – of 'giving back' – is not always realistic for people experiencing poverty. This raises critical questions about how charitable food aid can evolve in the future. How can it prioritise rights, not charity? What do transformations in charitable food aid look like? And perhaps most importantly, who gets to decide?

7

Mechanisms for Ending
Charitable Food Aid

Charity can only ever be a temporary fix to food insecurity. Under a right to food framework, food insecurity is viewed as a failure of the system, not something that should be addressed through charity alone. Enshrining the right to food in domestic law could provide essential social protections for those whose needs are currently unmet. But for a right to food framework to be truly effective, it must be considered alongside broader policy solutions that ensure social protections, such as cash-first approaches or UBI. Workers' rights and legislation are also part of the broader picture of ensuring people can access food with dignity.

'CASH-FIRST' APPROACHES

The term 'cash first' was originally popularised in Scotland by the A Menu for Change project,[1] a collaboration of anti-poverty charities dedicated to demonstrating that food insecurity was rooted in people's lack of income.[2] Overall, cash-first approaches aim to address the root causes of food insecurity by providing the financial means for individuals to secure their own food, promoting long-term solutions rather than temporary fixes. If fulfilled, the approach would result in everyone being able to access a living income through adequate social security payments and wages, as well as cash payments in times of crisis. It also focuses on prioritising advice, including signposting people to local support to maximise their income. Charitable support then becomes the last resort.

Where charitable support *is* needed, cash first calls for this to be made via cash, shopping vouchers or gift cards instead of food

Cash First: Ending the need for charitable food aid

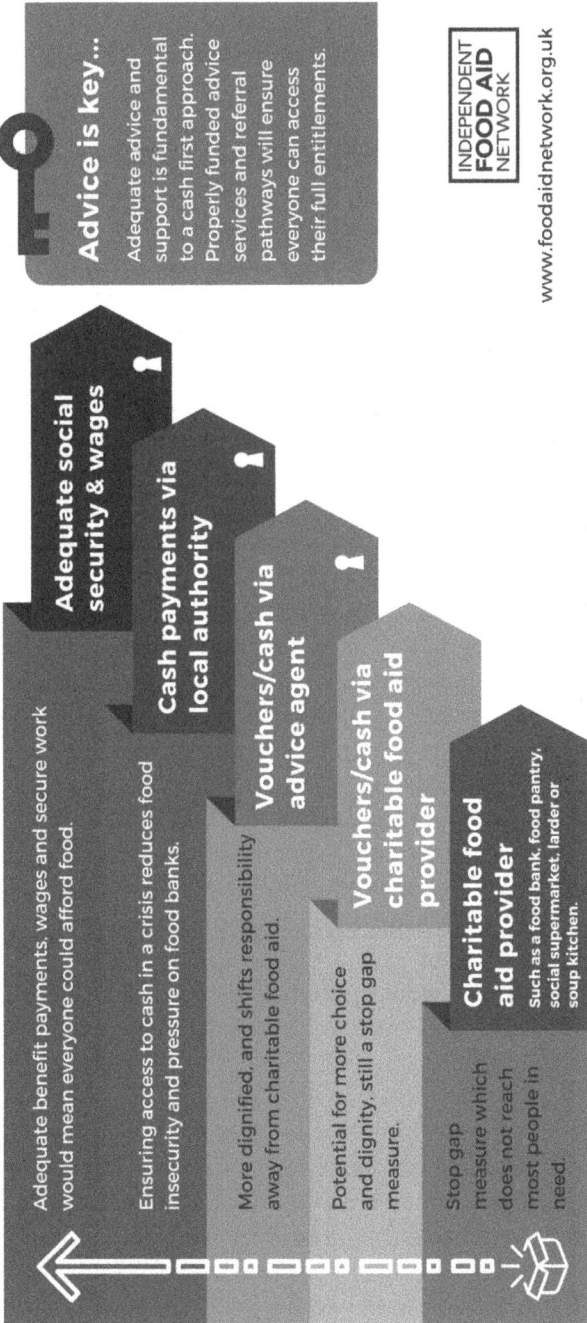

Advice is key...

Adequate advice and support is fundamental to a cash first approach. Properly funded advice services and referral pathways will ensure everyone can access their full entitlements.

INDEPENDENT **FOOD AID** NETWORK

www.foodaidnetwork.org.uk

Adequate social security & wages

Adequate benefit payments, wages and secure work would mean everyone could afford food.

Cash payments via local authority

Ensuring access to cash in a crisis reduces food insecurity and pressure on food banks.

Vouchers/cash via advice agent

More dignified, and shifts responsibility away from charitable food aid.

Vouchers/cash via charitable food aid provider

Potential for more choice and dignity, still a stop gap measure.

Charitable food aid provider

Such as a food bank, food pantry, social supermarket, larder or soup kitchen.

Stop gap measure which does not reach most people in need.

Figure 1   Cash First: Ending the Need for Charitable Food Aid (IFAN)

Source: www.foodaidnetwork.org.uk/infographics

parcels. In the UK, IFAN are staunch advocates for a cash-first approach to food insecurity (Figure 1). The network has worked with local and national partners to co-develop cash-first referral leaflets across more than 100 UK local authorities. Director of IFAN Sabine Goodwin and former project manager Maria Marshall write that: 'To truly tackle food insecurity, we need structural change to prevent financially induced crises from happening in the first place, not just to respond to them. However, when it comes to reversing the institutionalisation of charitable food aid, how crisis support is provided at a local level matters a great deal.'[3]

Trussell have also been trialling a cash-first approach. An evaluation of their pilot with Leeds City Council found that the majority (86 per cent) of people who received a cash grant didn't use a food bank in the period they received grant instalments.[4] Households were texted a PIN code they could type into a cash machine to receive the money, which was then spent on items such as food, gas and electricity. In a report published in June 2023, the Scottish government made history when it set out its human rights-based approach to ending the need for food banks.[5] This approach includes a focus on dignity and ensuring that people's right to food is met, with a particular emphasis on providing cash-first support rather than relying on food aid. In doing so, they became the first government worldwide to commit to the eradication of charitable food aid. But as Goodwin has pointed out, food banks represent a fraction of the community-driven charitable food provision on offer. 'The aim is clearly not to end the need for food banks while other gap-filling charitable food support measures proliferate', she said.[6]

It is important to work through some potential misunderstandings of the cash-first concept. I asked Sabine to explain some of these misconceptions:

People sometimes think that we mean cash being given out by a food bank. This can be action taken as a step on the ladder to help people in the here and now, but ultimately cash first is not about food banks giving out cash, vouchers, or gift cards. It's about food banks being in a position to evolve into other types of venue or to not exist at all because people have adequate incomes through their social security payments or wages, and that there's a system in place in every local authority for people to be able to access cash payments in a crisis if they need support.

In the pandemic, we saw how temporary cash boosts to people's incomes helped reduce food bank usage and food insecurity. In the US, changes in public assistance, including increased tax credits, funding for social programmes and food assistance, all helped reduce food insecurity.[7] The US Congress temporarily increased SNAP benefits in two ways: raising all benefits by 15 per cent and boosting every household to the maximum benefit for their household size. In April 2021, the USDA took action that increased benefits for all households by at least $95 to help very low-income families who already received the maximum benefit – or close to it – before the pandemic.[8] In the UK, a £20 uplift to UC saw a 16 per cent reduction in severe and moderate food insecurity, according to the government's own data.[9]

Although a cash-first approach can offer a more tailored and dignified approach, difficulties remain in resourcing it, including staff time and funding, especially given cuts to local authority budgets. There can also be barriers around digital accessibility. A Citizen's Advice Scotland shopping card pilot showed that some clients were unable to manage digital cards and grants or collect physical cards, or had literacy difficulties.[10] Those living in rural areas may also struggle to obtain food via a cash-first approach, as their access to affordable, nutritious and culturally relevant food can be limited. Food provided in local shops is often prohibitively expensive compared to the bigger supermarkets, meaning cash-first provisioning may not extend as far in rural areas.

SOCIAL SECURITY FOR FOOD

In Belgium and France, collectives of NGOs, farmers, researchers and citizens are experimenting with the idea of 'social security for food', or *sécurité sociale de l'alimentation* (SSA). Inspired by their universal healthcare systems, the idea is that every citizen receives a monthly allowance to purchase food that meets specific environmental and ethical standards. In Brussels, an innovative pilot has been taking place at the Brussels Ecological, Economical Super-market (BEES) Co-op, the nation's first consumer-owned and managed supermarket. Launched in 2014 by members of Reseau ADES – a youth network advocating for democratic, social and ecological alternatives – BEES Co-op is located in Schaerbeek, one of the most diverse municipalities in the Brussels-Capital Region. Almost 37 per cent of Schaerbeek's inhabitants come from abroad, and around three-quarters of the inhabitants have a migration background.[11]

During my visit to BEES in October 2023, I learned more about this groundbreaking trial. Project manager Margherita Via told me that the social security for food pilot has helped the Co-op to become more integrated with the wider community. 'At first we talked about the inclusion of the co-operative within the neighbourhood – but the neighbourhood was already here.' Margherita's role is to work in solidarity and collaboration with the local community so BEES could integrate more fully and 'be what the community needs'. As part of the trial, 70 low-income house-holds in Schaerbeek received €150 per month to spend at the BEES Co-op. The pilot was funded through the social welfare centre, using public funds. Initially, it included participants aged 65 and older, before being extended to single mothers.

Participants were required to volunteer to work a monthly 2 hour and 45 minutes shift in the Co-op, just like other members. There were no restrictions on the products people could choose. Upon entering, trial participants scan their cards, which are the same as those used by all shoppers. 'It's not this label when you go to pay, it's the same card as everyone else', Margherita explained. Feedback so far had been positive. 'Finally, I don't have to eat the garbage of other people', participants have fed back to Margher-ita and the team. People enjoyed being able to choose quality food for themselves and their children. Mostly, they used their allow-ance on fruit and vegetables, rice and dairy products. Many single mothers would keep half their allowance to use at the end of the month when money was running low.

Why not just give people extra money, I asked? 'Giving money was not enough', Margherita replied. The pilot is also about foster-ing community and solidarity. 'It's been extremely enriching for us to become more involved in the community', Margherita told me. To do this, it's taken time to build up trust. They sent out flyers in different languages and hosted parties and dinners in the street. Unsurprisingly, they've found that money was the main barrier preventing people from coming to the Co-op before the pilot. Social life has improved significantly, especially for senior people in the pilot. It's also about access to high-quality products. Items at the Co-op are carefully selected and sold at relatively low prices, which Margherita recognised can still be too costly for people on a low income: 'Prices are low, but still huge for the income of the neighbourhood.'

The BEES Co-op intentionally does not sell Kellogg's, Coca-Cola or Nutella. 'These are symbols of capitalism', Margherita told me, 'and besides they are usually not that cheap'. They have set criteria for their product range. They never stock products from huge corporations that exploit producers, workers and the environment. Instead, there is always an alternative they can offer that is similar in price and taste. They don't want to be in competition with local grocers, so they don't serve Halal meat as people already have a favourite preferred butcher for that. On the day of my visit, the shelves were heaving with different types of sprouts, greens and seasonal vegetables which come from local farmers.

'It feels super violent to say your €150 is gone', Margherita told me as we discussed the pilot coming to an end in December 2023. They're encouraging people to continue being involved in Co-op and hope to extend the pilot to reach a bigger group of participants in Schaerbeek. The evaluation of the pilot suggests that the social security for food approach needs to be evaluated in urban, rural and regional settings, as needs will differ according to the specific requirements of communities. Like cash-first approaches, funding is expensive and requires political will. 'It's becoming more difficult to get funding', Margherita said as we reflected on the future of the trial. The public have the impression that 'there is already an abundance of food aid, so why should we give people money for food, too? I'm wondering if people are ready to accept it.'

Since 2017, momentum has been building in both Belgium and France around the social security for food concept. Jonathan Peuch, an advocacy officer for the right to food and nutrition at FIAN

Belgium, highlighted that 70 to 80 organisations are part of the CréaSSA Collective, which is actively promoting the approach.[12] In France, more than a dozen pilot projects have been completed in cities including Bordeaux, Montpellier, Lyon and Toulouse. Researchers Somhack Limphakdy and Juliette Gravis, who are studying the SSA in France, explain that the SSA concept draws inspiration from France's long history of mutual aid, which contributed to the establishment of the healthcare system after World War II and the self-organisation of the working class in welfare and healthcare. The SSA aims to promote food democracy and ensure access to quality food for all. While the initiative seeks to address the limitations of charitable food aid, including what anthropologist Benedicte Bonzi calls 'food violence',[13] it also focuses on strengthening the relationship between consumers and the agrifood sector.

What does that look like in practice? In Montpellier, the programme La Caisse Alimentaire Commune de l'Hérault, or the Common Food Bank, was launched in January 2023. Of the 300 people taking part in the trial, more than 50 per cent come from low-income groups. Everyone contributes funds to the Common Food Bank: some contribute €5, others €150, but everyone ends up with €100 each. 'This is how solidarity shows itself', Juliette said. I asked if there was resistance to contributing more than others. 'A sliding scale suggests that you self determine your contribution according to your wages', Juliette said. 'Right now, it is based on trust. If this were larger scale like the healthcare system, it cannot just be based on trust. It would be based on salaries and taxed'. The universal element of social security for food – where each person receives the same amount to spend on organic, local and quality food – has parallels with UBI.

UNIVERSAL BASIC INCOME(S)

Once viewed as a utopian philosophical concept, UBI has evolved into a serious policy discussion. While no country has fully implemented UBI on a nationwide scale, several pilots around the world have shown promising results. I asked UBI expert Dave Beck, lecturer in social policy at the University of Salford and co-chair of the UBILab Manchester, how he saw UBI fitting into a broader right to food framework:

> A regular, unconditional cash-based basic income, non-with-drawable and given as a right to every adult (and a smaller amount to every child), on top of any earnings, would lead to the closure of food banks. If the government (and by extension, charity) is serious about ending the need for food banks, then a UBI is that answer they are looking for. With more income, people could better afford food, maintain their rent, and bills, lower their debt, leading to an improved quality of life.

'This is not just utopian thinking', he continued. 'All the pilots of basic income that have happened across the world have shown positive benefits.' For example, the basic income trial in Stockton, California found that the largest proportion of basic income spending was on food, bills, consumables and transport to/from work and job interviews.[14] This challenges the idea that people would spend their money on 'wrong' priorities or that UBI acts as a disincentive to seek paid employment. In fact, a two-year UBI trial in Finland found that recipients did not significantly reduce their work hours. Instead, they were more inclined to pursue meaning-ful, stable jobs that were better suited to their skills. Although the trial didn't show any long-term impact on people's employment status, people reported being happier and generally had greater life satisfaction.[15] In the US, where there are currently more than 100 UBI pilots being explored or delivered, researchers have seen similar results.[16] By providing a baseline income to all, UBI can play a role in reducing income inequality. 'In India', Dave pointed out, 'one notable pilot has shown both poverty reduction, improve-ments in income, health and levels of education'. This trial, in Madhya Pradesh, showed a narrowing of the gap between those on the highest and lowest incomes.[17]

Canada has conducted two major basic income experiments in the last 50 years. The Mincome experiment took place in Manitoba from 1974 to 1979 and was designed by a group of economists who wanted to address rural poverty. The programme showed tangible results: over the four years it ran, an average family in Dauphin was guaranteed an annual income of CAD\$16,000.[18] Over four decades later, the Ontario Basic Income Pilot Project was introduced 'to test a growing view at home and abroad that basic income could provide a new approach to reducing poverty in a sustainable way',[19] according to the provincial government. The trial provided individuals with an annual income of about CAD\$17,000 (for single people) and CAD\$24,000 (for couples), regardless of employment status.

This project was intended to last for three years, from 2017 to 2020, but was cancelled in 2018 by the newly elected Conservative government. This provoked a class-action lawsuit brought forward by 4,000 people, which alleged Ontario breached the terms and conditions of the contract it entered into with participants.[20] Early findings from the trial suggested improvements in mental health, reductions in poverty-related stress and greater financial stability. Many participants reported being able to pursue education or better employment opportunities, with no significant drop in work participation. Elaine Power, a professor at the School of Kinesiology and Health Studies at Queen's University, has studied and advocated for UBI for many years. Elaine's book, *The Case for Basic Income: Freedom, Security, Justice*,[21] co-authored with journalist Jamie Swift, emphasises how an unconditional basic income not only means freedom from scarcity but also the freedom to decide what to do with your income, and also with your time.

During my visit to Toronto in May 2024, I witnessed first hand the growing momentum and enthusiasm for a basic income. Many discussions centred on how the core principles of UBI could end the need for charitable food aid. Nick Saul and Kathryn Scharf at Community Food Centres Canada talked about basic incomes, plural. Others spoke of a guaranteed liveable income or a basic income guarantee. Matt Noble, executive director of the Toronto Vegetarian Food Bank and creator of the national Put Food Banks Out of Business campaign,[22] also flags how a UBI could be implemented for people living in Indigenous communities:

Indigenous communities are nations. The government of Canada should not be the one to design a basic income for Indigenous communities. A total payment, based on a per capita amount (and an administrative payment), can be given to communities, on a predictable basis, which they can use in whatever way they deem best for the members of their communities. A basic income is by no means full or adequate compensation from Canada for everything that has been taken from Indigenous communities, but it's a predictable amount that would help to address poverty and food insecurity. It's the least Canada can do.

UBI is a tool that can and should be considered in working towards societies where people can choose the food they wish to eat. 'Even a modest UBI would be enough to ensure the Right to Food by providing everyone with the means to meet their basic needs, and I believe this would eliminate the need for food banks, rapidly', Dave Beck told me.

UNIVERSAL FREE SCHOOL MEALS

One prominent example of advocacy for universal free school meals in the UK is the campaign launched by footballer Marcus Rashford.[23] In 2020, he called for every child in a low-income family to be guaranteed a free school meal, effectively bringing the issue to a wider audience. The Food Foundation has estimated that 800,000 children in England are living in poverty but do not qualify for free school meals.[24] Scotland had promised to start offering free school meals to all primary school children, but the motion was defeated in September 2024 due to 'prolonged Westminster austerity and record high inflation'.[25] All primary school children in Wales can now access Universal Primary Free School Meals,[26] in response to rising cost-of-living pressures on families and the Welsh government's stated ambitions of tackling child poverty and ensuring no child goes hungry in school. Similarly, all primary school children in London also receive free school meals, a policy that benefits a larger number of children than in Wales. The London initiative has been in place since 2014 as part of the city's efforts to address food insecurity and support families in one of the UK's most unequal areas to live.

Universal free school meals for every child is the number one demand from the UK's national right to food campaign, led by Ian Byrne MP.[27] Currently, children are not able to access free school meals equally. Byrne notes how thousands of children with special educational needs and disabilities are missing out on the free school meals they are eligible for.[28] Moreover, the Sustain alliance have shown how many children, despite living in poverty, are not eligible for free school meals due to their family's immigration status or because of recent changes to eligibility requirements linked to UC.[29]

In the US, the movement for universal free school meals is gaining traction, following temporary policies implemented during the pandemic by the USDA which allowed children in many states to access free school meals for the first time. Marlene B. Schwartz and Juliana Cohen have explained how eight states – California, Colorado, New Mexico, Maine, Massachusetts, Michigan, Minnesota and Vermont – have chosen to provide free meals for all public school students since the USDA stopped funding universal free school meals after the 2021–2 school year.[30] The momentum brought about by the pandemic inspired greater advocacy and grassroots action around this issue. Jan Poppendieck, a scholar and activist on poverty, hunger and food assistance in the US, has urged:

> Advocates are gearing up for a fight for universal free school meals. Since these programs are so essential to the survival of low-income households, we cannot afford to miss the moment of heightened concern and consciousness created by the shared experience of the pandemic. Food justice activists should lend their considerable moral force and organizing skills to these fights to expand rights to food.[31]

Visiting Vancouver in May 2023, I was shocked to hear that Canada was the only G7 country without a national school meals programme.[32] In April 2024, then Prime Minister Justin Trudeau announced that the next federal budget would include CAD$1 billion over five years for a national school food programme. Launching it, Trudeau said:

The National School Food Program is a game changer. The Program will take pressure off of families, invest directly in the future of our kids, and make sure they're able to reach their full potential – feeling healthy and happy. This is about fairness and doing what's right for our kids to get the best start in life.[33]

Free school meals vary across Europe, but experts agree they are key to tackling childhood obesity and social inequalities.[34] Ultimately, across all rich-but-unequal countries, political will is essential in ensuring *all* children are able to access a free school meal.

WORKERS' RIGHTS AND LEGISLATION

Many of those working in the food system are experiencing food insecurity themselves. The Bakers, Food and Allied Workers' Union is the largest independent trade union in the UK's food sector. Over 60 per cent of respondents to their 2023 survey said their wages were not currently high enough to meet their basic needs.[35] Respondents also reported having to change their purchasing habits, with 80 per cent now buying cheaper food. Almost 17 per cent of the food workers who took part in the research had had to use a food bank themselves.

People working on the front line as food delivery workers – often in partnership with national hunger-fighting, anti-poverty charities – can be disproportionately impacted by food insecurity themselves. This is especially true for undocumented migrants with 'no recourse to public funds' working for online food platforms such as Uber Eats and Deliveroo.[36] The controversy surrounding Trussell's partnership with Deliveroo stems from the perceived ethical contradiction between the charity's mission and the practices associated with gig economy companies. Deliveroo is a prominent player in the gig economy, which has faced criticism over issues such as workers' rights, job insecurity, low pay and lack of benefits. In response to the criticism, Trussell has emphasised that the partnership is focused on the practical goal of addressing immediate food needs and that Deliveroo's logistical expertise can support their mission. Deliveroo pointed to its wider 'history of working with charities to provide meals to those in need', claiming their riders welcome 'the chance to determine their own work patterns and work when and where they want', and denying that riders earn less than the minimum wage. In May 2024, Trussell announced a two-year extension of the partnership,[37] raising concerns about the implications of such partnerships on worker rights and dignity.

Campaigns for a living wage often highlight the importance of secure, stable employment alongside fair wages. The gig economy and precarious work, where people have little job security and unpredictable incomes, are major contributors to food insecurity. Living wage campaigns frequently advocate for better working conditions, including reliable hours and full-time contracts, which can provide workers with the financial stability needed to avoid food banks. They advocate for wages that reflect the true cost of living, rather than merely the statutory minimum wage, which is often inadequate to cover basic necessities such as housing, food, utilities and transportation. Such campaigns can play a significant role in addressing the root causes of food insecurity and, ultimately, reducing or ending the need for charitable food aid.

In the UK, the Living Wage Foundation promotes the 'Real Living Wage', which is calculated based on living costs, rather than the government's National Living Wage, which can still leave people in poverty. When workers are paid a real living wage, they are less likely to experience food insecurity and have to seek out charitable food aid. In the US, the Next Shift campaign is calling for 'thriving' wages and safe, fair working conditions for all staff and workers in anti-hunger and hunger relief organisations.[38] Their campaign argues that food access organisations must embody their commitment to economic justice. In addition, they call for narrative change work to shift the conversation on food insecurity and charity towards solidarity and economic justice for all.

8

Advocating for Change and the Importance of Solidarity

'HOW DO YOU START TO CLOSE A FOOD BANK?'

The suggestion of alternative models is nothing new. For years, those in non-profit organisations working to end food insecurity have been trying to ensure their models offer more than just a place people can receive free food. Nick Saul and The Stop Community Food Centre in Toronto developed a pioneering approach to tackling food insecurity by transforming the traditional food bank model into a holistic community hub focused on addressing the root causes of poverty and hunger. Saul, who became the executive director of The Stop in 1998, recognised the limitations of traditional food bank models and sought to redefine the organisation's role. Under his leadership, The Stop evolved from a conventional food bank into a Community Food Centre – a place that not only provided food but also aimed to empower individuals and build community resilience.[1]

The Stop created programmes that went beyond food distribution. These included community kitchens where people could learn to cook nutritious meals, community gardens where they could grow their own food and advocacy programmes that encouraged participants to become activists for food justice. Treating people with dignity and fostering a sense of belonging was key to the success of the Community Food Centres model. The spaces were designed to be welcoming, with a focus on creating a community atmosphere rather than a charity model. After leaving The Stop in 2012, Saul and fellow food activists launched Community Food Centres Canada (CFCC). CFCC moves the target of advocacy from the local and provincial levels to the federal level, aiming to scale up the concept and model of community food centres through-out Canada. At the time of writing, there are 15 Community Food Centres, with 35 staff and a network of 300 other organisations.

I met CEO Nick Saul and Chief Program Officer Kathryn Scharf in the CFCC offices in Toronto. One of the first things Nick told me was how 'good or shitty community programmes won't solve food insecurity'. I was interested to hear from them about what other countries with less established food-banking models should do to avoid further institutionalisation of a model that effectively does not work. 'Don't say you're the answer. Focus on healthy food. And don't build more food banks', Nick stressed. 'We're public space builders', Kathryn added. 'People come [to CFCC] because it's fun and joyful.' If you build community centres based on the power of food, the 'emergency' side disappears, but 'public space lives, and lives in a fulsome way', she continued. This results in a 'political but also nurturing' place for food that is 'not gross and stigmatising'. At CFCC they moved away from measuring pounds of food given out and the number of donors and towards a model that instead measures healthy food access, well-being, a sense of belonging and civic engagement.

'How do you start to close a food bank?' Nick mused. 'The idea of starting again and putting the genie back in the bottle is a com-plicated one. I just wish people could be a bit more honest about the shortcomings [of emergency food].' The UK in particular offers an example of how charities are openly working towards ending the need for food banks altogether. Trussell and Joseph Rowntree Foundation's Essentials Guarantee would embed in the UK social security system the widely supported principle that, at a minimum, UC should protect people from going without essentials. The UK government would be required to set the level of the Essentials Guarantee at least annually, based on the recommendation of an independent process.[2]

Discussing the growth of food banking with Professor Michael Fakhri, the current UN special rapporteur on the right to food, he told me: 'Food banks advocating for change is powerful, like in the UK context.' The Stop and their subsequent CFCC model inspired Seb Mayfield to co-found IFAN in the UK, a network of independ-ent, grassroots food aid providers working together to ensure food

security for all, in 2016. After spending time in Canada researching alternative responses to food insecurity, Mayfield identified the
need for a national network of independent food aid providers,
bringing them together and giving them a powerful national voice.
Now, IFAN is a leading advocate for ending the need for food
banks through a cash-first approach, which would mean everyone
is able to access a 'living income' and a 'healthy standard of living
for all'. Taking a cash-first approach to food insecurity at a local
level means prioritising income-focused crisis support by means of
cash payments, or vouchers if cash payments aren't available, and
advice and support to maximise income.[3]

In early 2020, the Trussell network of food banks also committed
to ending the need for food banks in their five-year strategy. A key
part of this was Trussell's Pathfinder Programme, which involves
trialling new approaches in a number of food banks across the
UK. Currently, 55 food banks are participating, each committed to
developing a strategic plan tailored to their local context. According to Harry Johnson, the Pathfinder Programme Lead for Trussell
in Scotland:

> Food banks joining the programme are encouraged to think
> about their local activities under the three key areas of the
> Together for Change strategy: Changing Communities, Changing
> Policy, and Changing Minds. The programme initially focuses
> on three key areas: the involvement of people with lived expe-
> rience, improving referral pathways, and promoting financial
> inclusion.[4]

As part of the programme, each food bank receives an expanded
support package from Trussell. This includes access to flexible
grants designed to build strategic capacity and participation in
a unique series of events and residentials aimed at co-producing
solutions to hunger and poverty with local communities.

While food banks are traditionally seen as providers of emergency food, they can offer much more: a sense of community,
referrals to additional support and in some cases advocacy for
broader social change. In June 2023, Emma Revie, CEO of Trussell,
shared her insights with me about the future of food banks:

There may still be people who need to access food banks, but that doesn't have to mean emergency food. There will always be individuals who struggle, particularly those facing mental health challenges or isolation. So, as food banks consider their future role, they must think about how they evolve to meet these needs.

Meanwhile, new approaches to food insecurity are emerging, aiming to address its wider social and cultural dimensions. Models such as food clubs, community kitchens, social pantries and community gardens are offering alternatives to traditional charitable food aid. Bruckner and colleagues suggest that these new models are promising, as they challenge the neoliberal stigma around food insecurity and move closer to food justice.[5] Andrew Forsey, director of Feeding Britain, explained to me:

> When we consider the growing demand for support alongside the decline in donations – whether in food, money, or volunteer time – we cannot continue as we have. The need for help isn't going away, but we can't meet it in the same way we have over the past decade. That's why we're shifting towards a food club model. It offers a more dignified form of support because people have the dignity of choice and purchase. It also has the potential for sustainability, creating a virtuous circle where we can reinvest income back into food.

In September 2023, I asked Sabine Goodwin, director of IFAN, about how these alternative models fit into the broader conversation of ending the need for charitable food aid altogether. She told me:

> If a food pantry is not relying on charitable donations of any kind, on any grants or volunteer labour, and it's not using surplus food, and it can sustain itself through buying and selling food at low prices, it's basically a shop, isn't it? It's a community food project that's a shop. Then we can see ultimately how these types of projects could outlive the need for charitable food aid … But what I'm seeing right now are food pantries dependent on surplus food, charitable grants and volunteer labour proliferate

in the UK and there's a real misunderstanding as to what these venues actually represent. Far from addressing the root causes of poverty driving hunger, it's as if we are being pushed to take a detour off the road to ending the need for food banks. In fact, most pantries these days are what could be described as food banks in disguise. I think it's vital we're collectively open about the fact that there shouldn't be a need for any form of charitable food aid. Food bank teams aren't campaigning to end the need for their services so that other types of food aid providers take their place.

Reflecting what Nick and Kathryn told me at CFCC, Sabine continued:

These models are still a response to the fact that people can't afford to buy food or don't have the choice to buy food in the way that everyone else does. And yes, they provide more dignity and choice, and I'm not saying it's not a step up the ladder, because it is. But let's not think that they're the answer, because they are really not the answer. People should have the choice about any food venue they access. It shouldn't be a matter of using a food pantry because there's no alternative due to lack of income.

The conversation around these new models highlights the critical importance of framing access to food as a basic human right, rather than a charitable act. This perspective shifts the focus to dignity and sustainability in how we address food insecurity, urging us to move beyond temporary fixes and work towards lasting, systemic change.

During my visits to various organisations, I found a shared commitment to ensuring that food aid is experienced with dignity and free of stigma. This often meant providing fresh, organic and culturally appropriate food, as well as catering to special dietary needs. Equally important was the attention given to physical space – lighting, acoustics, layout and aesthetics – all designed to create an environment that promotes dignity and comfort.

I saw first hand how, even with the best intentions of staff and volunteers, arriving a few hours after opening often meant fewer options and less availability of food. The idea of equality – of everyone getting the same experience – was often undermined by the limited nature of resources. And then there's the challenge of relying on surplus food, which complicates the goal of dignity and stigma reduction. Giving people Christmas products in April is never going to make people feel like they're accessing food just like everyone else. At the same time, there are mutual aid approaches based on solidarity that rely on surplus but are able to foster an incredible, tangible sense of community. These models, though imperfect, have created spaces where people feel valued.

Moving forwards, it's crucial to nurture and expand these collective strategies of resistance, alongside advocating for new, more sustainable models that could eventually eliminate the need for charitable food aid altogether. The reality is that it's incredibly challenging to meet the ever-growing demand for help while also dedicating energy to advocacy and systemic change.

RESPONDING TO SCARCITY THROUGH FOOD SOLIDARITY

When I first set out on these visits, my aim was to learn directly from those who were working in innovative and creative ways to address food insecurity and poverty – both within and outside charity. A central part of this was exploring how grassroots food solidarity initiatives were responding to the everyday realities of food insecurity in rich-but-unequal countries. I wanted to understand what kinds of alternative practices were emerging on the ground and how these practices were shaped by broader social, political and economic pressures. More specifically, I was interested in how these collectives were building community and care through food, and whether they were able to challenge dominant narratives of charity, hierarchy and scarcity. I was also interested to explore the kinds of tensions and contradictions they might encounter in trying to do this work, day in, day out.

I had some awareness of the politics around surplus food before these visits, particularly debates around food waste as a symptom of systemic overproduction and inequality, but the visits brought these issues into much sharper focus. What stood out to me most was the emotional and material labour involved in sustaining these initiatives, and how frequently workers on the front line are forced to navigate the limits of what surplus food can offer. Being in those spaces and speaking with volunteers and organisers helped me better understand the lived complexities and contradictions of working with surplus food as a means of both care and critique.

On the same day that news of the King Charles Coronation project was reported in the UK, I was in Belgium visiting the Bouche à Oreille (BAO) collective in Brussels. Born in October 2020 as a solidarity response to the pandemic, BAO transforms 'unsold food' into free meals for people in precarious situations, operating on the basis of no hierarchy in order that everyone feel welcome and included. 'We didn't want to be just us cooking for people', explained Kim-Minh Pham, a founding member of the collective. BAO serves 120 to 150 people weekly, creating what Kim calls 'a culture of sharing, with everyone involved in the creation of that moment'.

Volunteers dedicate an average of 13 hours per week to BAO and its programmes. Volunteers sign a contract giving them access to €35 for four hours of volunteering a day, equivalent to €2,000 per year. 'This gives value to their time', Kim told me, 'but it's hard to ask people to keep going'. Kim himself gave about 15 hours a week to BAO. He told me he hadn't been to a distribution for around two months prior to my visit. When I asked why, he told me a huge amount of his time was taken up with administration and fundraising bids. Kim stressed that they need proper funding to expand and grow, but that this is difficult when relying on public funding: 'In the long run, we don't want to have to keep asking for this.'

We walked about five minutes to Place Flagey, following the volunteers as they pushed a wooden cart filled with meals. In the square, around 30 people had gathered – mostly older individuals and some who were homeless. Several vans were set up, such as La Bulle (The Bubble) which offered free washing machines, haircuts and coffee. Another van housed a mobile shower and a professional hairdresser. Nearby, social services staff – always the same faces – offered support. The aim, I was told, was to create a 'solidarity village'. The atmosphere was calm and familiar, unlike some of the other distributions I'd seen.

As we stood chatting at the distribution, Kim spoke of the difficulties of finding unsold food, especially with corporations such as Too Good to Go and Belgian app Happy Hours Market, both of which provide daily access to shops' unsold food just before they close at reduced prices, monetising the surplus food market. 'Most people who use these have money to buy food in the supermarket', Kim told me, which signals a broader issue of the diversion of surplus away from the working class to the middle class. 'We're working with unsold food for people who *really* need it.'

Something I hadn't anticipated was how apps such as Too Good to Go are impacting charities such as BAO, who rely on a steady supply of surplus food. Too Good to Go first launched in Europe in 2015 and the US in October 2020. Co-founder Lucie Basch says the app saves 300,000 meals a day from ending up in landfills around the world.[6] Tammara Soma at Simon Fraser University has pointed out the difficulty of an app being able to address 'the root causes of wastage and the need to change inefficient practices'. These apps can be useful in diverting food waste from a farm, store or restaurant, 'but it is not clear whether or not the final product will always be fully consumed by consumers or if they will end up going to the bin anyway'.[7] Often, the food is near the end of its shelf life. Happy Hours Market do give BAO 'their leftovers' but the vegetables are frequently past their best and can't be given out anyway. 'We were their garbage, you know?', Kim shrugged.

A few days later, I visited No Javel! in the Forst area of Brussels. I met Déborah Levy, a former volunteer turned employee, who explained the group's name. I'd Google translated it but the translation of 'No Bleach' didn't make any sense. She told me it did in fact mean 'No Bleach' – it was named as a response to retailers who were pouring bleach over surplus food in the bins outside their stores so people couldn't consume it. 'It was a cry, a shout against the retailers who were pouring bleach over their unsold food. Enough!'

Founded in 2016 by precarious young people, No Javel! is a grassroots response to food insecurity. 'We were created by poor people, for poor people', said coordinator Alice Berwart. Alice and her friends from the area were 'dumpster diving', sharing the food with friends at first. Most volunteers have been, or are, beneficiaries of the solidarity grocery store. Some people are really ashamed to come, so 'it's important for us to be able to say we have all been there, too', Déborah said. She started working at No Javel! as a volunteer two or three years ago, and openly told me she had experienced precarity and 'dumpster diving' herself. At the start of 2023, Déborah became an employee – 'being paid is dignity' is one of the key values underpinning their work. No Javel! is about coming together – whether as a worker, volunteer or beneficiary – in order to share good quality, healthy food.

The group distributes nearly 1,000 organic, vegetarian food boxes monthly, mostly to 1,000 registered households, and also to about 15 other food aid groups. 'Good food is not just for rich people', Déborah makes clear. The logistics of securing food is a constant balancing act. Déborah told me how they 'have already said no to some people as they were giving us trash'. When I asked what she meant by 'trash', she said 'super processed food, or food that has already gone bad'.

The volunteers flitted around the space like worker bees. Everyone had a role and was busy preparing, cleaning, packing and sorting. On the day I visited, there were around 15 volunteers of all ages sorting boxes filled with fresh produce from organic farms. There was music, shared food and a real sense of community. Volunteers carefully checked the food's quality – only about 10 per cent goes to waste. After distributions, the surplus is shared among volunteers, not as payment but as support. I looked on as Déborah prepared boxes with yoghurt, cheese and hummus. 'I have a salary and I wouldn't buy it', she said, pointing towards the expensive €5 vegan cheese. 'When I see the prices in the supermarket, I feel sheltered as I get most of my food from here. If people are fighting over cabbages [here], I see the prices in the shop and I understand.' Each box given out at the social grocery is worth around €50–60, and around 45 boxes will likely be handed out on the day of my visit. There were lots of carrots! They never know what they're going to get in advance and usually find out what's available either on the day of distribution or the day before. The carrots were laid out, along with fresh bread, on tables near the beginning of the line so people could take more of those items if they wanted, in addition to their prepared fruit and vegetable boxes. They used to let people choose their own items, but since the pandemic they switched to the boxes to make sure everyone has enough.

I'd been chatting to Déborah for around half an hour when the volunteers started arriving and a buzz began to fill the walls of the old glass factory. A laptop was set up with chilled dance music playing and volunteers started sorting through the food, carefully placing green beans and mushrooms into small brown paper bags. Huge shiny tomatoes, leeks and courgettes were added to the crates, alongside apples the workers and volunteers had picked themselves in Liege at the weekend. Solidarity and collectivist values is what keeps No Javel! going. There is always someone cooking in their little kitchen ahead of distributions, and they always make time to chat. I ate some of the vegetable pasta with tofu and some delicious homemade guacamole on fresh bread as I chatted to some of the volunteers. I spoke to a volunteer who described himself as 'a newcomer to Brussels', who had been working there for two years. 'It is unbelievable, the waste of the capitalist system. Tell everyone in your research!'

As we were finishing our lunch, I saw people turning up well ahead of their appointment time, despite efforts to introduce an appointment system with no queuing; 2 pm came and it was time for the distribution to start. Eight people can come in and receive their boxes every ten minutes. Each person has a membership card and Alice marks them down on her clipboard. Their kids play together in a play area. The distribution was swift, easy and hassle-free. People helped themselves to the free bread and carrots, and loaded all of the fresh, organic produce into the shopping trolleys they'd brought along with them.

Even though I spent just four hours at No Javel!, I got a real sense of the community and non-hierarchical space they were seeking to build. There are many other organisations I talk about throughout this book who are working hard to repurpose the best quality surplus food, opening up spaces for people to enjoy new flavours and eat nutritious and tasty meals together as a community. But as Alice said, 'it's not enough' to meet the needs of people who are living in poverty and insecurity. Just before I left, I asked Déborah if they would ever charge a nominal amount like some of the rescued food markets I'd encountered on my travels so far, in order to offer dignity to people accessing the food. 'Who are we to say where people will find dignity?' she replied.

MORAL ECONOMIES OF SCARCITY

The overlooked aspect of food waste recovery is not solely one of abundance. It also aligns with the logic of scarcity and contributes to a perception that some individuals are receiving more than others. My time at No Javel! brought the relationship between surplus food and the production of food scarcity into focus. Retailers apply bleach to food items because they want to prevent anyone from taking them without paying. People then receive food waste from retailers through organised and sanitised distribution methods that provide a facade of corporate social responsibility, along with the advantage of tax deductions. Queen Mary University of London academic Jon May and colleagues have suggested that charitable food aid in the UK is driven by 'a particular moral economy of scarcity designed to distinguish between those perceived to be deserving and undeserving', facilitated by years of government austerity ideology.[8] Even though the narrative surrounding food waste suggests we are generously reallocating 'surplus', we are also unintentionally perpetuating the problematic conditions of scarcity, despite there being an excess of food in the food system.

I witnessed the lived experience of scarcity on many occasions throughout the past few years. Early in March 2023, I was halfway through a two week visit to Rome to understand how organisations, researchers and communities are responding to poverty and food insecurity. I visited ReFoodGees, an organisation that redistributes up to a tonne of fruit and vegetables every Saturday from Nuovo Esquilino market. ReFoodGees got its name from the fact the organisation has refugees and asylum seekers among both its volunteers and beneficiaries, founder Viola de Andrade Piroli told me.

The people who come for food, as well as the volunteers, reflect Rome's diverse multiethnic Esquilino district, including those from North Africa, sub-Saharan Africa, Central and South America, Asia and Italy. Managed by a merchants' co-operative, the Nuovo

Esquilino market is made up of over 130 stalls offering a wide range of clothing, fruit, vegetables, meat, fish, rice, couscous and spices. ReFoodGees, in addition to recovering tons of food, seeks to maintain horizontality between volunteers and beneficiaries, providing food to anyone who shows up at the time of distribution without discrimination.

Like No Javel!, solidarity is a driving force. Everyone is able to access food as 'food waste is a problem for everyone', Viola told me. Around 60–80 people come to get food each week. I looked on as the queue began to form around 4.30 pm, ahead of the 5 pm distribution. People were checking their watches, fidgeting with their shopping trolleys. I was there with Francesca Benedetta Felici and Davide Marino, researchers from the Observatory on Poverty and Food Insecurity in Rome. We followed the volunteers in their high-vis vests around the market, asking the stalls for what they have left.

On our first walk around the market, very few vendors gave us anything – our trolley looked sad and bare. Francesca explained that the vendors wanted us to come back a little later so they knew what they had left, as there was still time to sell food before the market closed at 5 pm. On the second trip round the stalls, piles of greens, bananas, celery and cauliflowers were placed in the trolley, which was then taken outside, weighed and sorted for distribution by the volunteers. Some of the fruits and vegetables were discarded for use as compost as they weren't the best quality. If there's ever anything left, another organisation picks it up and cooks it, Viola said – although there is rarely anything left over.

Back outside in the queue, tensions were running high. I watched as the people queuing for food argued between themselves – someone had a bigger cauliflower; others have missed out on the crustless tramezzino sandwiches being passed around on a tray at the beginning of the distribution. At one point, a volunteer got involved in an argument with a guy who tried pushing to the front of the queue. There was almost a physical fight right in front of us, but another volunteer calmed the situation down – it was obvious he'd had to do this before. Later on, he told us the guy who queue jumped had a knife in his pocket. Racial tensions were openly evident, which shocked me. It all underlined the desperation of many of the people there, as well as the precarious situation the volunteers find themselves working in.

Ultimately, while solidarity-based food initiatives such as BAO, No Javel! and ReFoodGees are powered by values of solidarity and food justice, they are working within a dysfunctional food system that is ultimately designed to produce scarcity through its surplus and prevents these organisations from ensuring the very dignity and right to food they are seeking to offer.

MOVING TOWARDS FOOD JUSTICE

When we talk about tackling food insecurity and ending the need for charitable food aid, two big ideas often come up: rights and solidarity. A rights-based approach says that access to food is a fundamental human right – not something you should have to earn or qualify for. It demands that governments take responsibility, passing laws, building strong public systems and making sure no one goes hungry. But while this sounds powerful, in practice it can be slow, wrapped up in legal jargon and endless policy delays. It also needs significant political will. For people already facing hunger, it can feel distant and disconnected.

Solidarity, on the other hand, starts from the ground up. It's about people showing up for each other, sharing what they have and refusing to let anyone go without. This isn't about charity or handouts – it's about collective care and pushing back against systems that keep people hungry in the first place. From mutual aid networks to community kitchens and food co-ops, solidarity means acting now, together. But these efforts can be underfunded, overstretched and sometimes treated like a substitute for the kind of deep structural change that only governments can make.

Still, the most powerful movements are finding a way to do both, as we've seen throughout this book. They meet urgent needs with dignity and care, while also advocating for a world where food is a human right. That means challenging the systems – the corporate greed, broken welfare states and violent borders – that cause food insecurity in the first place. It means demanding rights *and* building radical alternatives. Rights without solidarity can become distant and bureaucratic. Solidarity without rights can risk burnout and fragility. But together, they can build the foundations of a different kind of future – one where food isn't a privilege but a guarantee, rooted in justice, community and shared power.

Working towards food sovereignty and solidarity in communities involves advocating for systemic changes in how food is produced, distributed and consumed, emphasising local control, justice and equity. It's about emphasising local control, culturally appropriate food and sustainable food systems, even in crisis situations. In practice, this means shifting away from top-down, externally driven charitable food aid approaches to more community-led responses based on solidarity and reciprocity. One example of how food banks, community food distribution sites and mutual aid organisations are contributing to progressively rebuilding local food and farm economies is by purchasing food directly from local farmers for redistribution through food banks. The US Farm to Food Assistance programme aims to connect local farmers with food assistance organisations.[9] By facilitating the donation of surplus produce, the programme helps support both agricultural viability and community nutrition, creating a sustainable system that benefits farmers, food banks and low-income families. An example of how this operates in practice is Zenger Farms and their CSA model, which pushes for local BIPOC farmers to be paid a fair wage, while ensuring those receiving the produce are able to access locally grown, culturally relevant food for themselves and their families.

NARRATIVE CHANGE

A significant aspect of advocating for a society where charitable food aid is no longer necessary is the work of changing narratives. As we've seen repeatedly throughout this book, charity shifts attention away from structural issues and leads to temporary, superficial fixes. It can depoliticise poverty and its root causes. New narratives as told by those volunteering and working on the front lines help to communicate the structural factors behind persistent hunger and poverty. These narratives can change the dominant public perception around solutions to hunger from one rooted in corporate-backed charitable food aid to one rooted in social justice and systems change. A key part of this is challenging false narratives that hunger and poverty are failures of the individual, and that food insecurity is separate from issues such as housing, health, education, economic justice, racism and human rights.

In September 2024, the UK's largest food bank franchise shortened its name from the Trussell Trust to Trussell in an attempt to improve accessibility and reduce barriers to those needing support. This first rebrand for 20 years introduced a new strapline of 'Ending hunger together', alongside updates to its logo, fonts, colours and visuals. Their brand refresh was co-designed with people with lived experience of poverty and food insecurity, as well as people working on the front line in food banks. How does that sit alongside their broader goals to end the need for food banks altogether? In June 2023, I asked Emma Revie, CEO of Trussell, what food banks could transition into:

Emma: We don't spend time thinking 'Who will Trussell Trust be?' Because Trussell Trust needs to be gone, in my opinion. Because we are a beacon of what is wrong. Now I might get challenged on that but it's always important to me. I think charities, it's very easy to get distracted from keeping the main thing the main thing. If you're thinking about your own self-perpetuation, it's dangerous. You can slide into something else. Whereas if you enter into partnerships, into collaborations, into strategy, this is not about our self-perpetuation. It's about what's right, it keeps you more focused. And I'm worried about anything less definitive.

Kayleigh: But what would happen then, because how many staff are part of Trussell Trust? So it's not an anti-poverty organisation, but you'd still be an organisation?

Emma: No, we shut down. And we've got to the point where we don't need us any more in the UK. That's 280 staff members that can go and get other work tackling other aspects of poverty, and we'll spend a necessary amount of time enabling that. There's no staff member who goes 'What will that mean for me?' So yeah, our staff are 100 per cent committed to that reality.

Ending hunger together forms the basis of the lobbying and organising approach taken by Susannah Morgan, then CEO of Oregon Food Bank in Portland, when I met her in May 2023. Ahead of visiting her, she shared her manifesto for food justice with me. The manifesto outlines what needs to happen – and what food bankers themselves need to be doing – in order to enable fundamental, systemic change that would see an end to the need for food banking altogether. The manifesto declares:

> So, food isn't a solution to hunger. Food is a solution to an empty plate, but it doesn't address the reason that someone needed to seek food assistance in the first place. Food prevents the physical experience of hunger for a short time. But it is not a solution …
>
> The food bank world still acts as if the quantity of food we distribute is related to the solution to hunger. That is why we set goals in terms of additional pounds of food collected/distributed. That is why we track gaps in terms of the number of 'missing meals'. Our warehouses get bigger and bigger. And in doing so, we promote the narrative that, if we only had enough food, we could solve hunger. We mislead our communities. And when our communities think that hunger can be solved with food, they don't search for the real causes of hunger – and work on real solutions.
>
> We are not solving hunger by focusing on food; we are prolonging hunger. Which makes us part of the problem.[10]

Tackling public policy is just one of the actions Susannah's manifesto urges. In Spring 2022, the Oregon Food Bank joined a coalition to rewrite Oregon's labour laws so that agricultural workers would be eligible for overtime.[11] Many of Oregon's agricultural workers are from Latinx backgrounds, often migrants or immigrants, both with and without documentation. Agricultural workers are some of the lowest paid workers in all of Oregon state, with most earning $25,000 or less per year – not even half the average income statewide – leaving many to face food and housing insecurity.[12] The legislation was successfully passed. 'Now that's tackling the root causes of hunger', the manifesto claims. 'If we aren't working on these policies – at the local, state and federal level – then we are not solving hunger.'

Starting discussions that frame food access as a human right rather than an act of charity is a crucial first step. Engaging individuals with lived experience in advocating for the right to food – rather than merely reforming charitable food aid systems – shifts the focus from temporary relief to ensuring sustainable, dignified access to food as a guaranteed right for all. To do this effectively – and meaningfully – it's essential to create policy spaces where people with lived experience feel respected and valued as equal partners. It's also important to prioritise people in communities experiencing food insecurity in decision-making processes, as only by involving those with lived experience in policymaking targeted at charitable food aid and the right to food can we hope to develop effective, equitable policies. When I'm talking about lived experience, I mean people who are accessing charitable and community food aid, as well as people who are volunteering and working on the frontlines. Food Power, a four-year programme of work delivered by the organisations Sustain and Church Action on Poverty, have produced a toolkit outlining what needs to be prioritised in order to achieve this:

- Choice: People having the ability to choose how and if they are involved, and the role they will play
- Voice: People having a voice, speaking for themselves, not just being listened to, but heard, valued and respected, even when people disagree
- Change: People having the ability to change something, building capacity to act, and work together as communities to do so
- Challenge: People having the ability to challenge the status quo and exercise their rights
- Confidence: People gaining confidence, believing in themselves, having a sense of control and independence and knowing that their experience is valued.[13]

The pace of the work is also a potential challenge – genuine collaboration and trust needs to be built up meaningfully over time, as David Coffin, head of participation at Trussell, told me:

> For us, the main challenge is pace, especially with the campaigns environment versus the slow and more deliberative pace that is needed for relationship building, creating trusting and open environments and genuine collaboration. Also, colleagues who may not have worked closely with experts by experience often need support, to work effectively in this way. It's very important to meet people as a whole person, and not a story or experience, as this work ultimately should be a solutions focused activity, that draws on the insights and knowledge gained through experience, and not be solely focused on that personal experience, for a whole number of reasons, including psychological safety and well-being.

Again, this work involves prioritising solidarity and community-based advocacy, which is time-consuming and not linear. Nevertheless, it is essential to imagining and realising societies where charitable food aid is a thing of the past.

CALL TO ACTION

Moving away from corporate-backed charitable food aid and towards income-based approaches to poverty and food security demands a shift rooted in solidarity, centred on three core actions.

Policy change is necessary to ensure that governments and corporations are held accountable for upholding the right to food and addressing the root causes of hunger and inequality. *Narrative change* is crucial for shifting public perceptions of food insecurity and building the political will for transformative action. Finally, *solidarity* is essential to building the collective power needed to challenge the structural inequalities that create food insecurity, both locally and globally.

Policy change

A right to food, if fully implemented and combined with measures that boost and protect income, could eliminate the need for charitable food aid in rich-but-unequal countries by addressing the systemic causes of food insecurity at their root. When food is recognised as a fundamental human right, governments are held accountable for ensuring all citizens have access to sufficient, nutritious and culturally appropriate food. This shifts the responsibility for addressing hunger from charities and individuals to the state. It is the state that must enact policies guaranteeing food security for all.

When a country recognises food as a fundamental right, it can create systemic changes that address the root causes of hunger. Countries including Brazil, Ecuador and Bolivia show that by combining legal frameworks, social protection, agricultural support and public food distribution systems, the need for charitable food aid can be significantly reduced, if not eliminated.[14] These countries demonstrate that the right to food can be more than a top-down, legal guarantee, but instead show how it can represent a comprehensive approach to ensuring long-term food security.

Right to food movements are gaining traction in many rich-but-unequal countries around the world as civil society, grassroots activists and policymakers increasingly recognise the importance of ensuring access to adequate food as a fundamental human right. As I've described, in the US there is a growing and powerful movement among civil society and grassroots organisers towards embedding right to food in state constitutions. Countries such as Germany, Scotland and Switzerland have developed and implemented constitutional amendments, national laws, strategies and policies that aim for the fulfilment of the right to food for all.

In the UK, many advocates for change are championing income-focused, cash-first approaches to addressing food insecurity, rather than solely focusing on the right to food.[15] Simply ensuring access to food is not enough; the underlying economic issues that contribute to hunger and food insecurity must also be tackled. The right to food then goes hand in hand with cash-first approaches. In practice, such an approach would compel governments to implement robust social safety nets that address poverty, unemployment, housing insecurity and wage inequality – the main drivers of food insecurity in wealthy countries. This means strengthening social safety nets, such as social security benefits and access to healthcare and housing, to address the root causes of poverty. It also means enacting policies that ensure real living wages and safe, stable working conditions for all workers. This is especially relevant when we consider those employed in the food industry, who are themselves often among the most vulnerable to food insecurity. Governments should also regulate corporate practices that contribute to food insecurity, such as the monopolisation of food production and distribution by a few large corporations, which drives up prices and limits access to affordable food for people living in low-income communities. These practices are driven by racial discrimination, particularly in the US, and also by gender and social class across rich-but-unequal countries.

Encouraging the general public to advocate for policy change around charitable food aid in rich-but-unequal countries is also a key element, and requires education, empowerment and accessible tools for taking action. One effective approach is the use of templates, such as IFAN's 'Write to Your MP' initiative,[16] which simplifies the process of lobbying policymakers by providing an easily downloadable template which can be filled in and shared with your local MP. The Put Food Banks Out of Business campaign offers a similar initiative in Canada. Their template letter is designed to be sent to MPs, federal party leaders and provincial representatives to make sure that a basic income is on their election policy platforms.[17]

All of the policy measures outlined above need to be supported by political will. Governments must do more than simply committing to fund the redirection of surplus food to food charities. The measures outlined here have the potential to tackle the institutionalisation of charitable food aid. However, to be sustainable in the long run, an effective, justiciable and enforceable legal framework is required. In the UK, the Labour government's commitment to establishing the 2010 Equality Act's socio-economic duty could provide a framework to reduce poverty and ensure the realisation of the right to food[18] – but this must include concrete actions to address poverty and inequality.[19]

Corporate accountability is a significant part of the necessary policy change required to end the need for charitable food aid. Corporations often position themselves as part of the solution to food insecurity by supporting food banks through donations of surplus food, financial contributions or logistical infrastructure. As we've seen, large multinational corporations such as Amazon may donate food or funds to food charities, yet they simultaneously contribute to the very conditions that drive food insecurity by paying inadequate wages, offering insecure or exploitative contracts, undermining labour rights and avoiding corporate tax responsibilities. Corporations must be held to account – for paying fair taxes, offering living wages, ensuring job security and upholding dignified working conditions across their operations and supply chains.

Corporate involvement often shapes dominant narratives about hunger, framing it as an issue of scarcity or charity, rather than justice and inequality. This narrative obscures the structural causes of food insecurity and depoliticises the debate, reducing public pressure for systemic reform – so corporations also need to be part of the second core action: narrative change.

Narrative change

Changing the narrative around food insecurity is perhaps one of the most important steps in moving from a charity-based approach to a rights-based one. As this book has shown, the dominant narrative often frames hunger as a problem to be solved via charity. Those who volunteer and donate to charitable food aid are badged as 'heroes', while those seeking food charity are often stigmatised as having made poor choices. Accessing food charity thus becomes an individual problem rather than a systemic issue rooted in inequality and injustice. This narrative upholds a framework that casts food insecure individuals as passive recipients rather than active citizens entitled to basic human rights.

Adopting a rights-based narrative recognises that food insecurity is a social and political problem that requires collective action to address it. We therefore need to advocate for a reframing of food security as a matter of social justice and human rights. Such a narrative shift is crucial for changing public perceptions of hunger and poverty, and building the political will to enact the policy changes needed to address food insecurity at its roots.

Research has shown that narrative change can be achieved through the stories and experiences of those most affected by food insecurity. Since 2008, Mariana Chilton, professor of health management and policy at Drexel University in Philadelphia, has collaborated with Witnesses to Hunger,[20] a research and advocacy project partnering with mothers and caregivers of young children who have experienced hunger and poverty. Through their photographs and stories, Witnesses advocate for their own families and others, seeking to create changes on a local, state and national level. When people who have experienced poverty speak out about the structural causes of their situation, they challenge the popular narrative of individual blame, shifting the focus to the broader social and economic forces that sustain food insecurity. This is why it's essential to centre the voices of those experiencing food insecurity in both policy debates and public discourse in a non-extractive and meaningful way.

Media and cultural representations of food insecurity also play a critical role in shaping public perceptions. Too often, media coverage of hunger focuses on sensational stories of charity and individual acts of kindness, while ignoring the systemic issues that create food insecurity in the first place. A rights-based narrative would shift the focus from charity to justice, highlighting the need for systemic change and holding governments and corporations accountable for their role in perpetuating hunger. Alison Cohen and Debbie DePoala have written about the shared stories that make up the dominant narrative of hunger in America, arguing that:

the cultural acceptance of hunger as something that will always be with us, the idea that it is up to good-hearted volunteers and generous corporate actors to address hunger through food drives and giving back at holidays, the personification of hunger as the nameless, faceless 'villain' that needs to be 'fought', the acceptance that hunger is an individual problem requiring an individual solution. These stories shape the dominant narrative that millions of us have accepted and spread since we were first instructed by our religious leaders, teachers and parents as early as kindergarten to bring in food from our own kitchen pantries to share with those less fortunate during the holiday season.[21]

Instead, we need new stories of mutual aid, food sovereignty and community-based solutions. Food security is not simply a matter of filling empty plates but is also tied to questions of agency, dignity and justice. Reframing hunger in this way involves reshaping public discourse around who deserves access to food and how that need should be met.

One important aspect of this shift involves changing the way food banks themselves communicate about hunger and poverty. Many food banks, bound by the constraints of their funding sources, reinforce narratives that de-emphasise the systemic nature of hunger. By highlighting stories of solidarity and the need for systemic change, food banks and advocacy groups can play a vital role in reshaping public understanding of food insecurity. Through shifting the narrative away from charity and towards rights, we can begin to dismantle the stigmatisation of those who experience poverty and food insecurity. Public support for food security policies is more likely to grow in a cultural context that understands hunger as an injustice that demands political, rather than charitable, responses. A fundamental component of achieving this is the collective power of building solidarity in reimaging societies without the need for charitable food aid in the first place.

The collective power of solidarity

The final element in rethinking the current dominant charitable food aid model involves a call for solidarity. True solutions to food insecurity require collaboration across sectors, linking food justice with movements for workers' rights, housing justice, healthcare and anti-poverty advocacy. As we've seen, food insecurity does not occur in a vacuum – it is connected to a host of other socio-economic issues. Addressing it requires solidarity that bridges these interconnected struggles, recognising that the struggle for food security is part of a broader effort to build a more just and equitable society.

Recognising the importance of solidarity and sharing experiences from the front line, I co-founded the GSA in 2018.[22] The

GSA is made up of people working and volunteering in charitable and community food aid spaces, national networks and grassroots activism, and academic researchers mostly based in rich-but-unequal countries in North America and western Europe. Our aim is to complement and amplify the work of grassroots networks and movements that are addressing food systems, public health inequities, poverty reduction and social security at the community, national, regional and global level. Much of our advocacy has focused on building collective strategies of resistance, as well as alternative models and practices that promote the right to food in our respective parts of the world.

It wasn't until April 2020 that we really started to galvanise our collective response to the pandemic. GSA members in North America working and volunteering on the front lines described how they felt they'd regressed back to the 1980s, when it was all about giving out food en masse. They felt the pandemic had caused them to lose their social justice framing as they scrambled to hand out food to lines of people waiting to receive it. Our monthly virtual meeting became a place of solidarity, where we could share what was working, what was challenging, and what could be done next. We worked together to co-develop horizontal organisational strategies for our collective:

- We engage our members in political education towards building a shared analysis across countries about the increasing use of charitable food aid, private philanthropy and transnational corporate food banking as a flawed response to hunger and poverty.
- We build or join in collective strategies of resistance and alternative models and practices to promote the fulfilment of the right to nutritious food in our respective countries and/ or provinces, cities or states.
- We amplify the voices, stories and experiences of those working to ensure the right to food for their communities; of those who are advocating for or implementing root cause solutions; and of those who are most impacted by hunger and poverty.

- We name and challenge the set of values, beliefs and stories, as well as the structures and institutions behind them, that uphold the false narratives that hunger and poverty are failures of the individual; that food insecurity is separate from other issues such as housing, health, education, economic justice, racism and human rights.
- We leverage our international perspectives and networks to commission and contribute to research that furthers rights-based and root cause solutions to hunger and poverty and to inspire and cultivate researchers to advance and deepen these scholarly practices.
- We particularly seek to develop research that builds connections across different geographies and between academia and grassroots collaborators.

In contrast to charity, the notion of solidarity offers a fundamentally different way of addressing food insecurity. Solidarity implies a relationship of mutual support and collective responsibility, rather than one of hierarchy and paternalism. Solidarity-based approaches to food aid seek to collaborate with communities, guided by values of reciprocity, love and care. As we've seen, these alternative approaches often emphasise local, sustainable food systems that prioritise food sovereignty – the right of people to control their own food systems – as a long-term solution to food insecurity.

Charitable food aid organisations themselves can be sites of solidarity if they move beyond the narrow mission of food distribution and engage in advocacy. As Alison Cohen, director of the US National Right to Food CoP explained, doing this work involves advocating collectively alongside each other:

In Iowa, where advocates attempted to influence the legislature to entertain a bill to amend the constitution to include the right to food, well, it's the 'bread basket' – so it has a long tradition of farming, but now commodity farming has really moved in there. What advocates and organisers are trying to do there now is base building. So they're saying, 'Let's get farmers and people who use food banks together to understand that their struggles are really the same, and start from there'.

By working alongside anti-poverty organisations, unions, farmers and housing advocates, food banks and charitable food aid organisations can amplify their impact, helping to address the root causes of the issues they encounter daily. Building alliances with these movements can transform food banks from temporary relief providers to active stakeholders in the pursuit of economic justice. But this takes time and energy – both of which are often in short supply for people working (often voluntarily) in food banks.

Finally, solidarity is essential in reshaping how we understand food aid on a global scale. Hunger is not just an individual problem but a consequence of global systems – economic policies, trade agreements and environmental changes – that often leave vulnerable communities exposed. A rights-based approach to food aid, grounded in solidarity, calls for international cooperation and collective action to address these global challenges. It demands that wealthier nations, which have historically benefited from exploitative trade practices and resource extraction in the Global South, take responsibility for contributing to global food security, not through charity but through policies promoting equity and justice in global food systems. While the right to food is often discussed in terms of dignity, equity and justice, it is also crucial that we work towards its recognition as a legal right. This means holding governments and institutions accountable for not only alleviating hunger but ensuring access to adequate, nutritious food as a matter of justice – where food security is seen as a right, not a privilege.

Conclusion

After two and a half years, visiting over 90 organisations across six countries, spending more than 300 hours in food banks, food pantries, urban farms, Food Policy Councils, food co-ops and solidarity emporiums, the evidence is clear: charitable food aid, while perhaps alleviating immediate hunger, fails to address the root causes of food insecurity, which are structural and deeply embedded in social, economic and political inequalities. But it also showed me the incredible power and potential in alternative models and practices that promote dignity, fairness, and social justice. These models are based on solidarity and reciprocity, not power, conditionality and hierarchy.

A profound tension exists in societal responses to hunger that cannot be ignored. The more resources are invested in building bigger, better food banks – even those dedicated to offering choice, dignity and market-like displays – the more this risks institution-alising charity as the answer to food insecurity. Each improvement to the charitable food system, while alleviating immediate hunger, diminishes the urgency for radical change. The most well-designed food bank still operates within a framework that treats food as gift rather than right, and recipients as beneficiaries rather than equals. This paradox confronts everyone working in this space: how to support people's immediate needs without entrenching the very systems that require transformation.

Corporate involvement in charitable food aid adds another layer to this tension. As major food corporations and retailers become increasingly embedded in charitable food systems through donations of surplus, sponsorships and governance, they gain reputational benefits while maintaining structural power over food systems. Framing food surplus redistribution as a win-win masks deeper structural failures. What looks like efficiency is often a way to manage waste without addressing why hunger exists in the first place. This hunger industrial complex allows corporations to appear as part of the solution while their business practices – such as exploiting cheap labour, monopolising food systems, contributing to environmental degradation and generating massive amounts of food waste – often contribute to the very conditions of poverty and food insecurity that necessitate charitable food aid in the first place.

This work took place in politically and economically turbulent times, in the aftermath of the pandemic, and across a Europe shaped by austerity, anti-migrant politics and deepening inequality. The weaponisation of food in Gaza – through the deliberate denial of food, water, land and humanitarian aid to Palestinians – not only constitutes a breach of international law, but also represents a profound and wholly devastating violation of the fundamental human right to food. The so-called refugee crisis, the war in Ukraine and the EU's neoliberal economic governance all formed part of the backdrop, shaping how food insecurity was discussed, managed and often depoliticised. This state of permacrisis became even more pronounced following the re-election of Donald Trump as US president in November 2024. In the US, food banks across the country, already strained by rising demand, say they will have less food to distribute because of at least $1 billion in federal funding cuts and pauses by the Trump administration.[1] In the UK, the Labour government elected in July 2024 has yet to implement policies that would see the end for charitable food aid, despite mentioning it in their manifesto. These ongoing crises expose the fragility and inadequacy of charity-based responses. They are not solutions. They are sticking plasters over structural wounds. But even in the midst of this failure, there is both resistance and hope. In food banks, community kitchens and grassroots spaces, people are building solidarity and refusing to accept hunger as inevitable. These acts – everyday, radical, collective – push back against the continued normalisation of food charity and demand a future built on justice, dignity and rights, not on corporate surplus.

What we need is a transformation in how we understand and address hunger.

This means:

- advocating for robust social policies that prioritise food security through income support and cash-based interventions;
- moving beyond corporate food charity models towards systems that address root causes;
- building horizontal, community-based networks where reciprocity replaces hierarchy; and
- organising collectively to challenge the narratives that normalise hunger.

Hunger is not inevitable. It is the result of decisions made without solidarity. The path forwards requires honesty about the limitations of charitable approaches and momentum to imagine alternatives. This won't be found in bigger and more efficient models of food charity but in reimagining our relationship to food, community and care. Rather than treating charitable food aid as a standard fallback response, we need to acknowledge it as a symptom of underlying systemic failures and instead build a society in which people only rely on charity in a true emergency. Doing so requires commitment from policymakers, energy from advocates and solidarity across communities. It involves rethinking long-standing practices and narratives, challenging entrenched interests, and envisioning a society that places human rights above corporate profits. Ending hunger will require more than temporary fixes – it demands lasting change to ensure that people no longer need to rely on charity and instead have access to food as a fundamental right, secured through solidarity and political will.

Notes

INTRODUCTION

1. The term 'rich-but-unequal countries' refers to nations with high overall wealth and economic development, yet which experience significant internal disparities in income and access to resources. Despite their wealth, large portions of the population still face poverty and inequality, often along lines of social class, race, gender, disability or geography.
2. Cohen, D. (2020) Help the hungry: middle-class graduates join food bank queues as crisis deepens. *Independent*, www.independent.co.uk/voices/helpthehungry/middle-class-food-poverty-london-b1769251.html (last accessed January 2025).
3. Butler, P. (2020) Growing numbers of 'newly hungry' forced to use UK food banks. *Guardian*, https://tinyurl.com/2ctj6ftb (last accessed January 2025).
4. Butler, P. (2024) How many people in the UK are in 'hunger and hardship'? *Guardian*, https://tinyurl.com/hwye2j5r (last accessed January 2025).
5. In 2024, the Trussell Trust, the UK's largest food bank franchise, rebranded themselves as 'Trussell'.
6. United States Department of Agriculture (USDA) (2025) Food security in the U.S. – key statistics and graphics, https://tinyurl.com/yb3vjtby (last accessed January 2025).
7. Statistics Canada (2024) Canadians are facing higher levels of food insecurity, https://tinyurl.com/erjah8f4 (last accessed January 2025).
8. Williams, A. and May, J. (2022) A genealogy of the food bank: historicising the rise of food charity in the UK. *Transactions of the Institute of British Geographers*, 47(3), 618–34.
9. Blyth, M. (2013) *Austerity: the history of a dangerous idea.* Oxford University Press.
10. Garthwaite, K. (2016) *Hunger pains: life inside foodbank Britain.* Policy Press.
11. Global Solidarity Alliance for Food, Health and Social Justice (no date) https://rightsnotcharity.org/.

12. Günel, G., Varma, S. and Watanabe, C. (2020) A manifesto for patch-work ethnography. *Member Voices, Fieldsights*, https://culanth.org/fieldsights/a-manifesto-for-patchwork-ethnography (last accessed January 2025).

13. Kane, A. (2024) Here's how much richer Bay Area billionaires got in 2024. (It's a lot). *San Francisco Standard*, https://sfstandard.com/2024/12/31/silicon-valley-billionaires-richer/ (last accessed January 2025).

14. Beckett, L. (2024) 'People don't like to see poverty': inside San Francisco's vicious race for mayor. *Guardian*, www.theguardian.com/us-news/2024/oct/22/inside-san-franciscos-brutal-and-expensive-race-for-mayor (last accessed January 2025).

15. Nassar, H. M. and Aslam, S. (2023) Vancouver tops Canadian cities in EIU liveability index. *City News Everywhere*, https://vancouver.citynews.ca/2023/12/27/vancouver-eiu-liveability-index/ (last accessed January 2025).

16. Burnett, K. (2014) Commodifying poverty: gentrification and consumption in Vancouver's Downtown Eastside. *Urban Geography*, 35(2), 157–76.

17. Skands, S. (2020) Microaggression and the consumption of poverty: a community's resistance to invasive walking tours in Vancouver's Downtown Eastside. Master's thesis, Queen's University, Canada, www.proquest.com/docview/2524386796?pqorigsite=gscholar&fromopenview=true&sourcetype=Dissertations%20&%20Theses (last accessed January 2025).

18. Bailey, S. and Richmond-Bishop, I. (2021) Food insecurity reveals baked-in institutional racism. *Sustain*, www.sustainweb.org/blogs/jun21-food-insecurity-reveals-baked-in-institutional-racism/ (last accessed January 2025).

19. Riches, G. (2018) Food bank nations: poverty, corporate charity and the right to food. Routledge.

CHAPTER 1

1. St Mary's Food Bank (no date) Mission statement, www.stmarysfoodbank.org/ (last accessed January 2025).

2. Riches, G. (1986) *Food banks and the welfare crisis.* James Lorimer & Company.

3. European Food Banks Federation (no date) Our story, www.eurofoodbank.org/our-story/ (last accessed January 2025).

4. Trussell (no date) End of year stats, https://cms.trussell.org.uk/sites/default/files/2025-05/eys_factsheet_uk_2025.pdf (last accessed January 2025).

5. I've been an IFAN trustee since 2018.

6. IFAN (no date) Mapping the UK's independent food banks, www.foodaidnetwork.org.uk/independent-food-banks-map (last accessed January 2025).

7. Baker, W., Knight, C. and Leckie, G.(2024) Feeding hungry families: food banks in schools in England. Working paper, https://tinyurl.com/359zpyc9 (last accessed January 2025).

8. Food Standards Agency (2024) FSA's flagship survey shows food affordability concerns have risen, https://tinyurl.com/5ds8dcss (last accessed January 2025).

9. The Global FoodBanking Network (no date) Our fiscal year 2023–2026 strategic plan, www.foodbanking.org/our-fiscal-year-2023-2026-strategic-plan/ (last accessed January 2025)

10. Costanzo, C. (2023) Mexican food bank earns world's first carbon credits for food rescue. *Food Bank News*, https://foodbanknews.org/mexican-food-bank-earns-first-carbon-credits-for-food-rescue/ (last accessed January 2025).

11. Ioanes, E. (2023) SNAP boosts kept millions out of poverty during Covid. Now they're gone. *Vox*, www.vox.com/policy/2023/3/4/23625015/snap-poverty-covid-benefits (last accessed January 2025).

12. Ray-Chaudhuri, S., Waters, T. and Xu, X. (2023) Poverty. The Institute for Fiscal Studies, https://ifs.org.uk/publications/poverty-chapter (last accessed January 2025).

13. Gov.uk (2020) £16 million for food charities to provide meals for those in need, www.gov.uk/government/news/16-million-for-food-charities-to-provide-meals-for-those-in-need (last accessed January 2025).

14. Power, M. (2022) Hunger, whiteness and religion in neoliberal Britain: an inequality of power. Policy Press.

15. CBC (2020) B.C. announces $3M in emergency funding to help struggling food banks, https://tinyurl.com/mr3j2pze (last accessed January 2025).

16. Warshawsky, D. N. (2023) Food insecurity and the Covid pandemic: uneven impacts for food bank systems in Europe. *Agriculture and Human Values*, 40(2), 725–43.

17. Arnold, M. and Vladkov, A. (2022) On the breadline: inflation overwhelms Europe's food banks. *Financial Times*, www.ft.com/content/

bb098ccd-c74b-4c7e-8baa-e90546030fa5 (last accessed January 2025).

18. The Trussell Trust (2023) *Hunger in the UK report*, https://hub. foodbank.org.uk/wp-content/uploads/2023/06/2023-The-Trussell-Trust-Hunger-in-the-UK-report-web.pdf (last accessed January 2025).

19. Trussell Trust (no date) Latest statistics, www.trussell.org.uk/news-and-research/latest-stats (last accessed January 2025).

20. UK Government (2023) Family resources survey: financial year 2022 to 2023, www.gov.uk/government/statistics/family-resources-survey-financial-year-2022-to-2023 (last accessed January 2025).

21. Gregory, A. (2025) Hospital admissions for lack of vitamins soaring in England, NHS figures show. *Guardian*, www.theguardian.com/society/2025/jan/01/hospital-admissions-lack-of-vitamins-iron-nhs-figures (last accessed January 2025).

22. Lambert, G. (2023) Thousands of people admitted to hospital suffering from malnutrition. *The Times*, www.thetimes.com/article/times-health-commission-thousands-of-people-admitted-to-hospital-suffering-from-malnutrition-n23hqgzjr?shareToken=5344 c9dc98f82745c8dd243ff4e20dc8 (last accessed January 2025).

23. Joseph Rowntree Foundation (2023) *Destitution in the UK 2023*, www. jrf.org.uk/deep-poverty-and-destitution/destitution-in-the-uk-2023 (last accessed January 2025).

24. Butler, P. (2022) Fresh fruit and veg given to low-income families in UK trial. *Guardian*, www.theguardian.com/business/2022/nov/22/fresh-fruit-and-veg-given-to-low-income-families-in-uk-trial (last accessed January 2025).

25. Feeding America (2023) Feeding America urges bold, collective action in face of increase in food insecurity, www.feedingamerica. org/about-us/press-room/usda-food-security-2023#:~:text=In%20 2023%2C%20the%20Feeding%20America,meals%20to%20 neighbors%20facing%20hunger (last accessed January 2025).

26. Brown, G. and Brown, S. (2023) The multibank and how to create one, https://gordonandsarahbrown.com/wp-content/uploads/2023/03/The-Multibank-and-How-to-Create-One.pdf (last accessed January 2025).

27. Stewart, H. (2023) 'What do we want? £15!' Hundreds join Amazon picket line for Black Friday strike. *Guardian*, https://tinyurl. com/34s6hm8d (last accessed January 2025).

28. Butler, S. (2023) Amazon's main UK division pays no corporation tax for second year in a row. *Guardian*, https://tinyurl.com/24aater3 (last accessed January 2025).

29. Martin, D. (2005) John van Hengel, 83, dies; set up first food bank in U.S. *New York Times*, www.nytimes.com/2005/10/08/us/john-van-hengel-83-dies-set-up-first-food-bank-in-us.html (last accessed January 2025).

CHAPTER 2

1. Waste and Resources Action Programme (no date) Actions to reduce food and drink waste, www.wrap.ngo/taking-action/food-drink/actions (last accessed January 2025).

2. Rethink Food Waste through Economics and Data (no date) In the U.S., 38% of all food goes unsold or uneaten – and most of that goes to waste, https://tinyurl.com/3p923va2 (last accessed January 2025).

3. Suaréz Peña, A. C. (2023) Food banks: an unsung hero of climate action. *The Global FoodBanking Network*, https://tinyurl.com/yc23kcj6 (last accessed January 2025).

4. The Global FoodBanking Network (no date) Reducing food loss and waste, www.foodbanking.org/reducing-food-loss-and-waste/ (last accessed January 2025).

5. Mackenzie, S. (2023) King Charles III appears on Big Issue magazine cover to launch food poverty project. *Big Issue*, www.bigissue.com/news/king-charles-big-issue-cover-rankin-coronation-food-project/ (last accessed January 2025).

6. Hallows, R. and Barton, A. (2023) King Charles never throws away cake in crusade against food waste. *The Telegraph*, www.telegraph.co.uk/royal-family/2023/10/22/king-charles-never-throws-away-cake/ (last accessed January 2025).

7. Ferguson, D. (2023) 'Obscene': anger after cost of King Charles's coronation revealed. *Guardian*, www.theguardian.com/uk-news/2024/nov/21/obscene-anger-after-cost-of-king-charless-coronation-revealed (last accessed January 2025).

8. Goodwin, S. (2023) UK's food poverty crisis is spiralling out of control – and there's only one way to fix it. *Big Issue*, www.bigissue.com/opinion/food-poverty-crisis-waste-uk-ifan-sabine-goodwin/ (last accessed January 2025).

9. Feedback (2025) Used by: how businesses dump their waste on food charities, https://tinyurl.com/ycxcz4pe (last accessed April 2025).

10. FareShare (no date) Provide grant support for surplus redistribution from farms, https://tinyurl.com/4scm8rwr (last accessed January 2025).
11. Savage, M. (2024) Chef Tom Kerridge calls on UK government to fund surplus food scheme. *Guardian*, www.theguardian.com/environment/2024/oct/27/chef-tom-kerridge-calls-on-uk-government-to-fund-surplus-food-scheme (last accessed January 2025).
12. Written evidence submitted by FareShare, https://committees.parliament.uk/writtenevidence/123804/pdf/ (last accessed January 2025).
13. Papargyropoulou, E., Fearnyough, K., Spring, C. and Antal, L. (2022) The future of surplus food redistribution in the UK: reimagining a 'win-win' scenario. *Food Policy*, 108, 102230.
14. Riches, G. (2021) Canada must eliminate food banks and provide a basic income after COVID-1. *University of British Columbia Magazine*, https://magazine.alumni.ubc.ca/2021/community-health/canada-must-eliminate-food-banks-and-provide-basic-income-after-covid-19 (last accessed January 2025).
15. Chrisafis, A. (2016) French law forbids food waste by supermarkets. *Guardian*, www.theguardian.com/world/2016/feb/04/french-law-forbids-food-waste-by-supermarkets (last accessed January 2025).
16. Mourad, M. (2022) Did France really ban food waste? Lessons from a pioneering national regulation. In S. Busetti and N. Pace (eds), *Food loss and waste policy*, 109–23. Routledge.
17. California Association of Food Banks (no date) SB 1383: grocery recovery, www.cafoodbanks.org/member-portal/sb-1383/ (last accessed January 2025).
18. Haider, A. and Roque, L. (2021) New poverty and food insecurity data illustrate persistent racial inequities. *American Progress*, https://tinyurl.com/mcrpau9d (last accessed January 2025).
19. Food and Agriculture Organization of the United Nations (no date) LEG – Law No 166/2016, also called the Gadda Law, https://tinyurl.com/4kst5et8 (last accessed January 2025).
20. Sisters (no date) The Council of Ministers approves on Tuesday the draft law that will oblige restaurants to inform customers that they can take leftovers with them, according to EL PAÍS, https://sistersproject.eu/new-law-on-prevention-of-food-losses/ (last accessed January 2025).
21. Wood, Z. (2022) Asda employees 'skipping meals' due to monthly payroll errors. *Guardian*, www.theguardian.com/business/2022/jul/

15/asda-employees-skipping-meals-monthly-payroll-errors (last accessed January 2025).

22. Banco Alimentare Roma (no date) Chi Siamo [Who we are], www.bancoalimentareroma.it/chi-siamo/ (last accessed January 2025).

23. I was asked not to name any companies, so I've deliberately used anonymous terms like 'a big company' to respect what was asked of me.

24. A type of Italian sweet bread and fruitcake, originally from Milan, and usually prepared and enjoyed for Christmas.

25. Fisher, A. (2017) *Big hunger: the unholy alliance between corporate America and anti-hunger groups*. MIT Press.

26. An Italian herbal liqueur that is commonly consumed as an after-dinner digestif.

27. Silverman, G. (2023) 'Emergency feeding' in America: making words and deeds actually matter. In M. Caraher, J. Coveney and M. Chopra, (eds), *Handbook of Food Security and Society*, 324–32. Edward Elgar.

28. Harwood-Baynes, M. (2023) People paying higher prices at big chains' smaller stores. *Sky News*, https://news.sky.com/story/people-paying-higher-prices-at-big-chains-smaller-stores-12865142 (last accessed January 2025).

29. Toth, A. (2024) Warning to convenience store shoppers over cost of essentials like milk. *Independent*, www.independent.co.uk/news/uk/home-news/tesco-milk-warning-which-local-stores-prices-b2619995.html (last accessed January 2025).

30. Bychawski, A. (2022) Modern-day Scrooges: corporations give 'small change' in charity stunts. *Open Democracy*, www.opendemocracy.net/en/amazon-coca-cola-christmas-donations-scrooge/ (last accessed January 2025).

31. About Amazon Team (2023) How we're supporting communities throughout the EU and UK, https://tinyurl.com/mtdj9438 (last accessed January 2025).

32. Sainato, M. (2023) 'They're more concerned about profit': Osha, DoJ take on Amazon's gruelling working conditions. *Guardian*, https://tinyurl.com/2tsxdb9c (last accessed January 2025).

33. Kollewe, J. (2024) Amazon workers in 20 countries to protest or strike on Black Friday. *Guardian*, www.theguardian.com/business/2024/nov/25/amazon-protest-strike-black-friday (last accessed January 2025).

34. Jordan, D. and Conway, Z. (2023) Amazon strikes: workers claim their toilet breaks are timed. *BBC News*, www.bbc.com/news/business-64384287 (last accessed January 2025).

35. Ungoed-Thomas, J. and Nonyelum Anigbo, N. (2023) Exhausted Amazon staff fight back against retail giant at global UK summit. *Guardian*, https://tinyurl.com/bdcu6d85 (last accessed January 2025).

36. Quinn, I. (2024) Is there too much competition among surplus food waste charities? *The Grocer*, https://tinyurl.com/26w5kupn (last accessed January 2025).

37. European Food Banks Federation (no date) The second life of food, thanks to Costa Cruceros and Banc dels Aliments, https://tinyurl.com/42787btv (last accessed January 2025).

CHAPTER 3

1. Trussell (2024) End of year food bank stats, www.trussell.org.uk/news-and-research/latest-stats/end-of-year-stats (last accessed January 2025).

2. Levkoe, C. Z., Stiegman, M., Rotz, S. and Soma, T. (2024) Colonialism, starvation and resistance: how food is weaponized, from Gaza to Canada. *The Conversation*, https://theconversation.com/colonialism-starvation-and-resistance-how-food-is-weaponized-from-gaza-to-canada-241525 (last accessed January 2025).

3. Martin, K. S. (2021) *Reinventing food banks and pantries: new tools to end hunger*. Island Press.

4. Hands on Hartford (no date) About Hands on Hartford, https://handsonhartford.org/about/about-2/ (last accessed January 2025).

5. Martin, K. S. (2021) *Reinventing food banks and pantries: new tools to end hunger*. Island Press.

6. Cohen, A., Garthwaite, K., Goodwin, S., guthrie, j. and Heipt, W. (2021) Food banks and charity as a false response to hunger in wealthy but unequal countries: global network for the right to food. In Global Network for the Right to Food and Nutrition (ed.), *Right to food and nutrition watch*, issue 13, *Not our menu: false solutions to hunger and malnutrition*. FIAN International, 20–5, www.righttofoodandnutrition.org/wp-content/uploads/2021/10/rtfn_watch13-2021_eng_web.pdf (last accessed January 2025).

7. Lipps, B. and Ibach, G. (2023) USDA ensures food, funding during pandemic. USDA, https://tinyurl.com/b9sn5cth (last accessed January 2025).

8. Personal email correspondence, Andy Fisher, 2 July 2024.

9. Government of Canada (2020) Government of Canada rolling out $100M in added support to food security organizations during

COVID-19 pandemic, https://tinyurl.com/52j7ye2w (last accessed January 2025).

10. The Food Foundation (2022) Government data shows £20 uplift is likely to have protected people on Universal Credit from food insecurity, https://tinyurl.com/3xknzsnt (last accessed January 2025).
11. Warshawsky, D. (2023) Food insecurity and the Covid pandemic: uneven impacts for food bank systems in Europe. *Agriculture and Human Values*, 40(2), 725–43.
12. Food Research and Action Center (no date) SNAP emergency allotments and public health emergency: addressing the hunger cliff, https://frac.org/programs/supplemental-nutrition-assistance-program-snap/emergency-allotments (last accessed January 2025).
13. Tampone, K. (2022) Syracuse leads the U.S. with worst child poverty among bigger cities, census says, https://tinyurl.com/mvarz5n7 (last accessed January 2025).
14. Lakhani, N. (2021) 'The food system is racist': an activist used a garden to tackle inequities. *Guardian*, www.theguardian.com/environment/2021/may/25/karen-washington-garden-of-happiness-us-food-system (last accessed January 2025).
15. Meyersohn, N. (2020) How the rise of supermarkets left out black America. *CNN Business*, https://edition.cnn.com/2020/06/16/business/grocery-stores-access-race-inequality/index.html (last accessed January 2025).
16. West Virginia University (2024) Food deserts and food insecurity in West Virginia, https://tinyurl.com/y4tpyf7u (last accessed January 2025).
17. Chew, A., Moran, A. and Barnoya, J. (2020) Food swamps surrounding schools in three areas of Guatemala. *Preventative Chronic Disease*, 17, 200029.
18. Wright, A. (2023) The movement to stop dollar stores from suffocating Black communities. *Capital B News*, https://capitalbnews.org/dollar-stores-black-communities/ (last accessed January 2025).
19. Hanson, K. L., Coupal, S., Grace, E., Jesch, E., Lockhart, S. and Volpe, L. C. (2024) Mutual aid food sharing during the COVID-19 pandemic: case study of Tompkins County, NY. *Public Health Nutrition*, 27(1), e215.
20. Dhillon, S. (2021) 'The greatest threat to the internal security of the USA': the Black Panther Free Breakfast for Children program. *Medium*, https://dsdhillon.medium.com/the-greatest-threat-to-the-internal-security-of-the-usa-the-black-panther-free-breakfast-for-e797636c5f94 (last accessed January 2025).

21. Potorti, M. (2017) 'Feeding the revolution': the Black Panther Party, hunger, and community survival. *Journal of African American Studies*, 21(1), 85–110.
22. Himmelstein, D. U., Lawless, R. M., Thorne, D., Foohey, P. and Woolhandler, S. (2019) Medical bankruptcy: still common despite the Affordable Care Act. *American Journal of Public Health*, 109(3), 431–3.
23. Walker, C., Schan, H., Devlin, B., Plowman, D. and Wise, M. (2022) *Hunger trauma: understanding experiences of food insecurity and emergency food support*. Adur & Worthing Food Partnership, https://awfood.org.uk/wp-content/uploads/2022/09/Hunger-Trauma-Report_compressed.pdf (last accessed January 2025).
24. Chilton, M. (2024) *The painful truth about hunger in America: why we must unlearn everything we think we know – and start again*. MIT Press.
25. The Chicago 'L' (short for 'elevated') is the rapid transit system serving the city of Chicago and some of its surrounding suburbs in the US state of Illinois.
26. Cherone, H. (2023) What does it mean that chicago is a sanctuary city? Here's what to know. *WTTW News*, https://tinyurl.com/33sw7kyf (last accessed January 2025).
27. Center for Immigration Studies (2018) Sanctuary cities fact sheet, https://cis.org/Fact-Sheet/Sanctuary-Cities-Fact-Sheet (last accessed January 2025).
28. Bunn, S. and Rolker, H. (2022) Diet-related health inequalities. *POST*, https://post.parliament.uk/research-briefings/post-pn-0686/ (last accessed January 2025).
29. The Rockefeller Foundation (2024) The Rockefeller Foundation to increase investment in U.S. food is medicine solutions to $100 million, https://tinyurl.com/4zadezv5 (last accessed January 2025).
30. Costanzo, C. (2024) NC food bank expects $24M in 'food is medicine' revenue. *Food Bank News*, https://foodbanknews.org/nc-food-bank-expects-2m-mo-in-food-is-medicine-revenue/ (last accessed January 2025).
31. Ibid.
32. Wilton, E. (2024) Press release: charity urges all parties to commit to national fruit and veg on prescription programmes. Alexandra Rose Charity, https://tinyurl.com/cbpu322j (last accessed January 2025).
33. Tarasuk, V. and McIntyre, L. (2022) Reconsidering food prescription programs in relation to household food insecurity. *The Journal of Nutrition*, 152(11), 2315–16.

34. Izumi, B. T., Martin, A., Garvin, T., Higgins Tejera, C., Ness, S., Pranian, K. and Lubowicki, L. (2020) CSA Partnerships for Health: outcome evaluation results from a subsidized community-supported agriculture program to connect safety-net clinic patients with farms to improve dietary behaviors, food security, and overall health. *Translational Behavioral Medicine*, 10(6), 1277–85.

CHAPTER 4

1. Name anonymised.
2. Glaze, B. (2017) Foodbank volunteers 'perform £30million a year worth of unpaid work', shock study reveals. *Mirror*, https://tinyurl.com/mw8vty8n (last accessed January 2025).
3. Dickinson, M. (2019) *Feeding the crisis: care and abandonment in America's food safety net*. University of California Press.
4. European Food Banks Federation (no date) Donate, https://tinyurl.com/4x4zsmj7 (last accessed January 2025).
5. Dickinson, M. (2019) *Feeding the crisis: care and abandonment in America's food safety net*. University of California Press, 96.
6. Spring, C., de Souza, R. and Garthwaite, K. (2024) Surplus food and the rise of charitable food provision. *Oxford Research Encyclopedia of Food Studies*, https://tinyurl.com/42dncb3v (last accessed January 2025).
7. De Souza, R. (2019) Feeding the other: whiteness, privilege, and neoliberal stigma in food pantries. MIT Press, 99.
8. martinez, j. (2023) Recommendations for the Emergency Food Assistance Program WSDA Food Assistance. *Future Emergent*, https://tinyurl.com/3up2ubra (last accessed January 2025).
9. Dickinson, M. (2019) *Feeding the crisis: care and abandonment in America's food safety net*. University of California Press.
10. White, C. (2024) *The food bank paradox and how to balance objectives: a case study*. The Independent Food Aid Network, www.foodaidnetwork.org.uk/post/the-food-bank-paradox-and-how-to-balance-objectives-a-case-study (last accessed January 2025).
11. Butler, P. (2023) UK food banks bring in counsellors and private GPs to help exhausted workers. *Guardian*, https://tinyurl.com/4mdf3dwb (last accessed January 2025).
12. Independent Food Aid Network (2022) Our joint letter to the prime minister, www.foodaidnetwork.org.uk/post/joint-letter (last accessed January 2025).

13. San Francisco-Marin Food Bank Union (2020) The workers at San Francisco-Marin Food Bank have ratified their first contract! https://sfmfoodbankunion.org/ (last accessed January 2025).

14. McDede, H. (2023) Alameda County food bank workers vote to unionize. *Oaklandside*, https://oaklandside.org/2023/11/08/alameda-county-food-bank-workers-vote-to-unionize/ (last accessed January 2025).

15. Freedom 90 (no date) Freedom 90 Charter, https://onelmon.com/freedom90charter.pdf (last accessed January 2025).

16. Closing the Hunger Gap (2022) Next shift: charity to solidarity – a narrative change campaign toolkit, https://tinyurl.com/2wrvbmr8 (last accessed January 2025).

17. Cohen, A., Garthwaite, K., Lohnes, J. and Wolpold-Bosien, M. (2023) *Rights, not charity: a human rights perspective on corporate food aid*, https://tinyurl.com/3wer5ff2 (last accessed January 2025).

18. Personal email correspondence, March 2024.

19. Walker, C., Devlin, B., Erickson, M., Schan, H. and Hanna, P. (2025) *Managing hunger trauma in community food support: systemic betrayal, moral injury and distress in staff and volunteers.* Alliance for Dignified Food Support, www.alliancefordignifiedfoodsupport.org.uk/moral-injury (last accessed January 2025).

CHAPTER 5

1. Boyle, K. and Flegg, A. (2022) The right to food in the UK: an explainer. Briefing: Economic, Social and Cultural Rights Part Four, https://tinyurl.com/2t8ududf (last accessed January 2025).

2. Office of the United Nations High Commissioner for Human Rights (OHCHR) (2012) Fact sheet no. 34: the right to development, www.ohchr.org/sites/default/files/Documents/Publications/FactSheet34en.pdf (last accessed January 2025).

3. OHCHR (no date) Key aspects of the right to food, www.ohchr.org/en/food (last accessed January 2025).

4. Namkung, V. (2023) UN hunger expert: US must recognize 'right to food' to fix broken system. *Guardian*, https://tinyurl.com/2bdu5tbd (last accessed January 2025).

5. House of Commons Environment, Food and Rural Affairs Committee (2023) *Food security: eleventh report of session 2022–23.* UK Parliament, https://publications.parliament.uk/pa/cm5803/cmselect/cmenvfru/622/report.html (last accessed January 2025).

6. Namkung, V. (2023) UN hunger expert: US must recognize 'right to food' to fix broken system. *Guardian*, https://tinyurl.com/2bdu5tbd (last accessed January 2025).

7. US National Right to Food Community of Practice (no date) www. righttofoodus.org/ (last accessed January 2025).

8. Roosevelt, E. (1958) 'Where do universal human rights begin?', statement on 27 March 1958 at the presentation of the book *In your hands: a guide for community action* to the UN Commission on Human Rights, www.ohchr.org/sites/default/files/Documents/Publications/Human_rights_indicators_en.pdf (last accessed January 2025).

9. Byrne, I. (no date) Right to Food campaign, www.ianbyrne.org/righttofood (last accessed January 2025).

10. Scottish Government (2023) 'Cash-first: towards ending the need for food banks in Scotland': plan, www.gov.scot/publications/cash-first-towards-ending-need-food-banks-scotland/ (last accessed January 2025).

11. European Citizen's initiative (no date) Good food for all, www.goodfoodforall.eu/ (last accessed January 2025).

12. Franklin, S. (2010) Belo Horizonte: the city that ended hunger. *Civil Eats*, https://civileats.com/2010/04/12/belo-horizonte-the-city-that-ended-hunger/ (last accessed January 2025).

13. Institute of Development Studies (2023) Brazil's return: towards zero hunger (again), www.ids.ac.uk/opinions/brazils-return-towards-zero-hunger-again/ (last accessed January 2025).

14. *Economist* (2023) Brazil's new president wants to reduce the number of hungry people, www.economist.com/the-americas/2023/01/19/brazils-new-president-wants-to-reduce-the-number-of-hungry-people (last accessed January 2025).

15. Rexine, E. (2023) This time around Brazil can and must do the anti-hunger fight right. *IPES Food*, https://ipes-food.org/this-time-around-brazil-can-and-must-do-the-anti-hunger-fight-right/ (last accessed January 2025).

16. Elver, H. (2023) Right to food. *Journal of Agricultural and Environmental Ethics*, 36(4), 21.

CHAPTER 6

1. Garthwaite, K. (2016) Stigma, shame and 'people like us': an ethnographic study of foodbank use in the UK. *Journal of Poverty and Social Justice*, 24(3), 277–89.

2. Spring, C., Garthwaite, K. and Fisher, A. (2022) Containing hunger, contesting injustice? Exploring the transnational growth of food-banking and counter responses before and during the COVID-19 pandemic. *Food Ethics*, 7(1), 6.
3. De Souza, R. T. (2019) *Feeding the other: whiteness, privilege, and neoliberal stigma in food pantries*. MIT Press.
4. Haynes Stein, A. (2023) Barriers to access: the unencumbered client in private food assistance. *Social Currents*, 10(3), 207–24.
5. Brown, F. (2024) Who is Lee Anderson? The MP who's become Reform UK's first MP. *Sky News*, https://tinyurl.com/37mw8rn5 (last accessed January 2025).
6. Think Money (2024) It's National Food Bank Day! – How you can spread the love, www.thinkmoney.co.uk/blog/it-s-national-food-bank-day/ (last accessed January 2025).
7. The Global FoodBanking Network (2023) Celebrating the Faces of Food Banking, www.foodbanking.org/blogs/thank-a-food-banker/ (last accessed January 2025).
8. Closing the Hunger Gap (no date) https://thehungergap.org/ (last accessed January 2025).
9. Voices of Hunger West Virginia (no date) Towards the right to food, www.voicesofhungerwv.com/new-page (last accessed January 2025).
10. Joseph Rowntree Foundation (2021) Is universal basic income a good idea? www.jrf.org.uk/social-security/is-universal-basic-income-a-good-idea (last accessed January 2025).
11. Gwilym, H. and Beck, D. (2023) Universal basic income: Wales is set to end its experiment – why we think that's a mistake. *The Conversation*, https://tinyurl.com/bdf5uhht (last accessed January 2025).
12. Wilson, N. and McDaid, S. (2021) The mental health effects of a universal basic income: a synthesis of the evidence from previous pilots. *Social Science & Medicine*, 287, 114374.
13. Put Food Banks Out of Business (no date) www.putfoodbanksoutofbusiness.com/ (last accessed January 2025).
14. PROOF (2024) New data on household food insecurity in 2023, https://tinyurl.com/394mbtw4 (last accessed January 2025).
15. Spring, C., Garthwaite, K. and Fisher, A. (2022) Containing hunger, contesting injustice? Exploring the transnational growth of food-banking and counter responses before and during the COVID-19 pandemic. *Food Ethics*, 7(1), 6.
16. Bruckner, H. K., Westbrook, M., Loberg, L., Teig, E. and Schaefbauer, C. (2021) 'Free' food with a side of shame? Combating stigma

in emergency food assistance programs in the quest for food justice. *Geoforum*, 123, 99–106.

17. The names throughout this example have been changed to protect anonymity.
18. Brinklow, A. (2024) SF plans more housing, but not everywhere. why the Tenderloin isn't on the map. *Frisc*, https://tinyurl.com/nhbh9ukz (last accessed January 2025).
19. Nourish Scotland (2024) Public diners: the idea whose time has come, https://tinyurl.com/2canytab (last accessed January 2025).
20. Ibid, 21.
21. La Via Campesina (2003) Food sovereignty: explained, https://tinyurl.com/4rm7ryp4 (last accessed January 2025).
22. US Food Sovereignty Alliance (no date) Food sovereignty, https://usfoodsovereigntyalliance.org/what-is-food-sovereignty/ (last accessed January 2025).
23. Chicagoland Food Sovereignty Coalition (no date) What is the Chicago Food Sovereignty Coalition? www.chifoodsovereignty.com/about (last accessed January 2025).
24. Gordon, C. (2024) Learning mutual aid: food justice public pedagogy and community fridge organizing online. *Journal of Applied Communication Research*, 52(2), 158–78.

CHAPTER 7

1. A Menu for Change (no date) Tackling food insecurity in Scotland, https://amenuforchange.wordpress.com/ (last accessed January 2025).
2. Independent Food Aid Network (no date) Taking a cash first approach to food insecurity, www.foodaidnetwork.org.uk/why-cash-first (last accessed January 2025).
3. Goodwin, S. and Marshall, M. (2024) Building 'cash first' momentum while breaking the food bank paradox from the ground up. Child Poverty Action Group, https://tinyurl.com/389vpwf7 (last accessed January 2025).
4. Gopal, K. (2022) Cash grants beat food vouchers. *Big Issue North*, www.bigissuenorth.com/news/2022/11/cash-grants-beat-food-vouchers/#close (last accessed January 2025).
5. Scottish Government (2023) Cash-first – towards ending the need for food banks in Scotland: plan, https://tinyurl.com/4bk327rj (last accessed January 2025).

6. Goodwin, S. (2023) Could food banks be relegated to the history books? *Big Issue*, www.bigissue.com/opinion/could-food-banks-be-relegated-to-the-history-books/ (last accessed January 2025).
7. White House (no date) The American rescue plan, www.whitehouse.gov/wp-content/uploads/2021/03/American-Rescue-Plan-Fact-Sheet.pdf (last accessed January 2025).
8. U.S. Department of Agriculture (no date) SNAP benefits: COVID-19 pandemic and beyond, https://tinyurl.com/mrhkce4e (last accessed January 2025).
9. The Food Foundation (2022) Government data shows £20 uplift is likely to have protected people on Universal Credit from food insecurity, https://tinyurl.com/3xknzsnt (last accessed January 2025).
10. Citizens Advice Scotland (2024) Food insecurity pilot: piloting short-term crisis support alongside holistic advice, https://tinyurl.com/2fcyerw6 (last accessed January 2025).
11. Stape Urban Consulting (2022) Cooperating like bees, https://tinyurl.com/5bdswwpr (last accessed January 2025).
12. CréaSSA Collective (no date) Decide collectively what's on our plate, www.campagne-ssa.be/en/our-topics/food-democracy/ (last accessed January 2025).
13. Bonzi, B. (2023) Food aid, a factor of resistance for a food democracy. *Multitudes*, 92(3), 86–94.
14. Treisman, R. (2021) California program giving $500 no-strings-attached stipends pays off, study finds. National Public Radio, https://tinyurl.com/4x8mnbcu (last accessed January 2025).
15. Malinka, J., Mitte, K. and Ziegler, M. (2024) Universal basic income and autonomous work motivation: influences on trajectories of mental health in employees. *Applied Research Quality Life*, 19(4), 1967–96.
16. Ferguson, D. (2024) Money for nothing: is universal basic income about to transform society? *Guardian*, www.theguardian.com/society/article/2024/jul/14/money-for-nothing-is-universal-basic-income-about-to-transform-society (last accessed January 2025).
17. Schjoedt, R. (2018) India's basic income experiment. *Development Pathways*, https://tinyurl.com/328z3pt4 (last accessed January 2025).
18. Cox, D. (2020) Canada's forgotten universal basic income experiment. BBC, www.bbc.com/worklife/article/20200624-canadas-forgotten-universal-basic-income-experiment (last accessed January 2025).
19. Ontario Basic Income Pilot (no date) www.ontario.ca/page/ontario-basic-income-pilot (last accessed January 2025).

20. CBC News (2024) Ontario government facing class action suit for abruptly cancelling basic income program, www.cbc.ca/news/canada/ toronto/basic-income-pilot-ontario-cancellation-lawsuit-1.7149067 (last accessed January 2025).
21. Swift, J. and Power, E. (2021) *The case for basic income: freedom, security, justice.* Between the Lines.
22. Put Food Banks Out of Business (no date) www.putfoodbanksout ofbusiness.com/ (last accessed January 2025).
23. Butler, P. (2021) Rashford demands a 'meal a day' for all school pupils in need. *Guardian*, https://tinyurl.com/4fv4uuv6 (last accessed January 2025).
24. The Food Foundation (no date) Health equals: supporting free school meals to reduce health inequalities for children, https:// tinyurl.com/22csx9c6 (last accessed January 2025).
25. BBC News (2024) Scottish government defeated in free school meals vote, www.bbc.co.uk/news/articles/ckg5vxe3v5eo (last accessed January 2025).
26. Welsh Government (2024) Universal Primary Free School Meals, www.gov.wales/universal-primary-free-school-meals-upfsm (last accessed January 2025).
27. Byrne, I. (no date) Right to Food Campaign, www.ianbyrne.org/ righttofood (last accessed January 2025).
28. Byrne, I. (2024) More than 100,000 eligible disabled children are unable to access the free school meals: the government must act. *Left Foot Forward*, https://tinyurl.com/bxm6nrcp (last accessed January 2025).
29. Sustain (2020) Briefing paper: free school meals and immigration policy, www.sustainweb.org/reports/free_school_meals_immigration_ policy/ (last accessed January 2025).
30. Schwartz, M. B. and Cohen, J. (2024) Free school meals are on the rise in the US – but that could change depending on who wins the 2024 presidential election. *The Conversation*, https://tinyurl. com/46e275yx (last accessed January 2025).
31. Poppendieck, J. (2022) Reformist, progressive, radical: the case for an inclusive alliance. *Canadian Food Studies/La Revue canadienne des études sur l'alimentation*, 9(2), 53–63.
32. The G7 is an informal group of industrialised democracies that meet annually to discuss global economic governance, international security and other issues and comprises Canada, France, Germany, Italy, Japan, the United Kingdom, and the United States.

33. Prime Minister of Canada (2024) A National School Food Program to set kids up for success, www.pm.gc.ca/en/news/news-releases/2024/04/01/national-school-food-program-set-kids-success (last accessed January 2025).

34. *Guardian* (2023) Pizza, plum cake and pickled red onion: how school lunches look across Europe, www.theguardian.com/society/2023/oct/13/about-stimulating-children-how-school-lunches-look-europe (last accessed January 2025).

35. The Bakers Food and Allied Workers Union (2023) Foodworkers on the breadline, www.bfawu.org/wp-content/uploads/2023/05/BFAW-Survey2023-Final.pdf (last accessed January 2025).

36. Mendonça, P., Clark, I. and Kougiannou, N. (2023) 'I'm always delivering food while hungry': how undocumented migrants find work as substitute couriers in the UK. *The Conversation*, https://tinyurl.com/3t233aw5 (last accessed January 2025).

37. Lepper, J. (2024) Deliveroo renews partnership with food charity. Better Society Network, https://tinyurl.com/48cknysn (last accessed January 2025).

38. Closing the Hunger Gap (2022) Next shift: charity to solidarity – a narrative change campaign toolkit, https://tinyurl.com/2wrvbmr8 (last accessed January 2025).

CHAPTER 8

1. Saul, N. and Curtis, A. (2013) The Stop: how the fight for good food transformed a community and inspired a movement. Melville House Publishing.

2. Trussell and Joseph Rowntree Foundation (2024) Guarantee our essentials: reforming universal credit to ensure we can all afford the essentials in hard times, https://tinyurl.com/ywbxv2n5 (last accessed January 2025).

3. Independent Food Aid Network (no date) Taking a cash first approach to food insecurity, www.foodaidnetwork.org.uk/why-cash-first (last accessed January 2025).

4. Personal email communication.

5. Bruckner, H. K., Westbrook, M., Loberg, L., Teig, E. and Schaefbauer, C. (2021) 'Free' food with a side of shame? Combating stigma in emergency food assistance programs in the quest for food justice. *Geoforum*, 123, 99–106.

6. Nowell, C. (2022) The apps fighting food waste by saving restaurant meals from the trash. *Guardian*, https://tinyurl.com/yuxdyajs (last accessed January 2025).
7. Ibid.
8. May, J., Williams, A., Cloke, P. and Cherry, L. (2020) Food banks and the production of scarcity. *Transactions of the Institute of British Geographers*, 45(1), 208–22.
9. Wallace Center (2024) Farm to food assistance: a model for values-based, equity-centered approaches to transforming the food system, https://tinyurl.com/5w4m4xbd (last accessed January 2025).
10. Morgan, S. (2023) *Food banking for justice: a manifesto*. Personal email communication, May 2023.
11. Oregon Food Bank (2022) We need farmworker overtime now! www.oregonfoodbank.org/posts/farmworker-overtime-2022 (last accessed January 2025).
12. Sierra, A. (2023) 'We are souls in the dark': farmworkers share Oregon housing challenges in new state report. *Oregon Public Broadcasting*, https://tinyurl.com/2ftdus68 (last accessed January 2025).
13. Pearson, B., Guerlain, M. and Shaw, S. (2020) Telling stories and shaping solutions: a toolkit for empowering people who have lived experience of food poverty. *Food Power*, https://tinyurl.com/243tpdfw (last accessed January 2025).
14. Food and Agriculture Organization of the United Nations (2020) Right to adequate food in constitutions, https://tinyurl.com/95eeaprc (last accessed January 2025).
15. Goodwin, S. and Marshall, M. (2023) Turning the tide: cash first and the right to food. IFAN, www.foodaidnetwork.org.uk/post/turning-the-tide-cash-first-and-the-right-to-food (last accessed January 2025).
16. IFAN (no date) Call on your MP to end the need for charitable food aid. www.foodaidnetwork.org.uk/write-to-your-mp (last accessed January 2025).
17. Put Food Banks Out of Business (no date) https://app.oneclickpolitics.com/campaign-page?cid=R5QCJZIBKqtrzFaES6wP (last accessed January 2025).
18. Just Fair (no date) The socio-economic duty. https://justfair.org.uk/campaigns-2/1forequality/ (last accessed January 2025).
19. Goodwin, S. (2024) Time is running out: the next government needs a proper plan to end reliance on food banks. *Big Issue*, https://tinyurl.com/mrx6nbcb (last accessed January 2025).

20. Center for Hunger Free Communities (no date) Witnesses to hunger. Drexel University, https://drexel.edu/hunger-free-center/projects/witnesses-to-hunger/ (last accessed January 2025).
21. Cohen, A. and DePoala, D. (2023) Stories matter: narrative change as a strategy for exposing the root causes of hunger and spurring collective action. In W. D. Schanbacher and W. F. Uy (eds), *Food insecurity*, 215–23. Bloomsbury Academic.
22. Global Solidarity Alliance for Food, Health and Social Justice (no date) https://rightsnotcharity.org/ (last accessed January 2025).

CONCLUSION

1. Brooks, B. (2025) USDA cuts over $1 billion in funding for schools, local food purchases, www.reuters.com/world/us/usda-cuts-over-1-billion-funding-schools-local-food-purchases-2025-03-11/ (last accessed April 2025).

Acknowledgements

It would be impossible to name everyone who supported the research for this book over the past few years. But I'm so grateful for the time and efforts of everyone who welcomed me into their communities and generously shared their experiences. I was often surprised by the number of people who responded to my out-of-the-blue emails, despite already dedicating so much care and labour to their charitable and community food aid work. Even when they didn't appear directly in the book, every visit shaped my thinking and understanding. Thank you all for taking the time to share the amazing work you're doing.

Whilst many friends and colleagues have supported this work in recent years, there are people I want to thank individually for their time, care, and support. Alison Cohen, Director of The National Right to Food Community of Practice in the US, has been a foundational part of this project. Since our first meeting in 2018, she has become a collaborator, road trip companion, host, and friend. Alison, along with Josh Lohnes, Research Assistant Professor at the West Virginia University Center for Resilient Communities, dedicated so much of their time to organising countless visits to organisations that I would have been unable to discover on my own.

Andy Fisher, author of *Big Hunger*, and his family kindly welcomed me into their home on my trip to the West Coast in May 2023. Francesca Benedetta Felici and her colleagues at CURSA, the Observatory on Food Insecurity and Poverty, hosted me in Rome for two weeks in 2023. Both Andy and Francesca spent hours facilitating visits and conversations with people who were working towards a system based on food justice and rights, not charity. Emily Mattheisen, formerly of FIAN International, hosted me on a trip to Heidelberg in May 2022, and worked hard to make sure our Bilbao gathering came together in November 2024. Sharing this experience with such thoughtful, kind, and committed colleagues – and now good friends – has been one of the most rewarding parts of this research.

The people who show up for the Global Solidarity Alliance for Food, Health and Social Justice (GSA) meetings every month have contributed to this book in one way or another. Meeting so many members in person during my field visits and in our joint trip to Bilbao have been particular highlights of the past few years spent researching for this book. Many of the memories we've shared together have been around realising our own right to food as we ate, drank, and got to know each other beyond a little square on a computer screen. A special thank you to David Lopategi at Bizilur for showing us around the beautiful Basque Country, where we not only ate and drank local specialties, but also learned about the solidarity initiatives working hard every day to uphold the right to food in their communities.

GSA members Alison Cohen, Andy Fisher, Sabine Goodwin, Josh Lohnes, Jan Poppendieck and Graham Riches all gave critical feedback on the early stages of my book proposal and later on draft chapters, encouraging me to refine my thinking and be bolder, which helped me massively. Jan and Graham have been like mentors to me since meeting them in Birmingham in 2018. As outstanding scholars with longstanding histories of work on charitable food aid, learning from them is a privilege. Alison and Sabine generously read the entire book from start to finish, offering careful feedback and encouragement. All errors are of course my own.

Without the time spent doing writing sessions with friends and colleagues Emily Ball, Frankie Rogan and Emma Watkins in the School of Social Policy and Society at the University of Birmingham, this book wouldn't exist. Their friendship, laughter, and shared snacks (virtual and otherwise) made even the longest writing days something to look forward to.

I am beyond thankful to the Leverhulme Trust for awarding me the Philip Leverhulme Prize in 2020 [PLP-2020-261]. Without the support of the Prize, the research and alliance building of the last few years wouldn't have been able to happen. The time away from teaching to focus on developing connections and conducting ethnographic fieldwork has been invaluable to me, and this book certainly wouldn't have been possible without it. Particular thanks to Bridget Kerr for her flexibility and support in extending the prize deadline, both due to pandemic disruptions and to allow for bereavement leave following the devastating loss of my lovely Gran in January 2022.

Working with the team at Pluto Press has been a pleasure. In particular, Ken Barlow supported the idea for this book from the very start, and Jonila Krasniqi, along with Ken, patiently worked with me to decide on a title that reflected what I wanted the book to say. I also want to say a huge thank you to the brilliant Kerry Hudson for writing such a powerful foreword which sets the tone for the book with sensitivity, care, and hope.

Finally, I have to thank my family for creating a space where I feel supported and able to write a book in the first place. Working away from home in places like New York City, Toronto and Rome was never something I imagined would be in my future, but Mam and my husband Craig helped me see I was capable of it. Mam has never stopped quietly pushing me forward and saw a researcher when I couldn't. Craig encouraged me to spend as long as I needed on my field visits and sometimes came along when he could. He curated playlists for the long drives that I shared with Alison across State lines. Our Friday night debriefs discussing what I was writing always helped me to make sense of what I was trying to say, and how I wanted to say it. He's always supported my independence while building the calm I came home to.

Index

INDEX

food donations as waste disposal
34–7
redlining by 59
Supplemental Poverty Measure (US) 23
Supplementary Nutrition Assistance
Program (SNAP) 23, 43, 56, 68,
100, 115
surplus food 29–36, 47–50
bleaching of 132, 135
as means of waste disposal 36–7
Sustain Alliance (UK) 122, 141
Swift, Jamie 120
Switzerland 92
Syracuse, NY 58–9

Tarasuk, Val 66
Tesco supermarkets 6, 38
Texas, migration to Chicago from 64
Too Good To Go (Belgium) 132
Toronto Vegetarian Food Bank 101
town fridges 60–1
Trudeau, Justin 122–3
Trump, Donald 90, 152
Trussell (formerly Trussell Trust) 3, 6,
21, 24–5, 51, 73, 77, 126–7,
139–40
and cash first system 114
links with Deliveroo 123–4
partnership with Asda 38
partnership with Morrisons 45
Pathfinder Programme 127

Uber Eats 46, 56, 68, 123
Ukraine 52
UN Committee on Economic, Social
and Cultural Rights 87–8
UN Covenant on Economic, Social
and Cultural Rights (ICESCR)
87–90
UN Human Rights Office of the High
Commissioner (OHCHR) 88
UN Special Rapporteurs 7
United States 143
Census (2021) 106
Covid-19 in 23, 115

declines to ratify ICESCR 89
Department of Agriculture (USDA)
26, 55, 115
Food and Agriculture Organization
(FAO) 7, 89, 108
healthcare in 62
United States food banks 2, 26–7, 152
Universal Basic Income (UBI) 100–2,
118–21
Universal Credit (UK) 23, 55–6, 115
Universal Declaration of Human
Rights (1948) 87
University of Bristol 21

Vancouver 12, 111, 122
Downtown Eastside 9–10, 12–13
Vancouver Neighbourhood Food
Networks (VNFN) 12
Via, Margherita 116–7
Voices of Hunger (US) 99–100
Voluntary Right to Food Guidelines
89, 92
volunteers 71–80, 82–4, 131, 133–4

Walker, Carl 62–3, 83
Walmart 33, 37, 54
Wardlaw, Reverend Robin 81–2
Warshawsky, Daniel 24, 56
Washington, Karen 59
Washington State Department of
Agriculture 74
Waste and Resources Action Pro-
gramme (UK) 55
West Side Campaign Against Hunger,
NY (WSCAH) 43, 50
West Virginia 59–60, 99–100
Which? magazine (2023) 45
White, Charlotte 75
Whole Foods Corporation 11
Williams, Andrew 4
Witness to Hunger project (US) 146
Wright, George 47

Zenger Farm, Oregon 67–8, 138
Zuckerberg, Mark 11